Growing Leaders with Sterling Integrators

By Ray Beerhorst

TO: PAUL,
I AM ENJOYING THE
PASSION YOU BRING TO
LEADING AGCO/GSI/IS
TO A MORE PROFITABLE
FUTURE!

Ray B.
04/18/2018

Contents

Who Are You and Why Does It Matter?

Make a Plan

A Tale of Two Leaders

The Traits of a Sterling Leader

Part I: What is Coaching and How Does It Work?

The Case for Leadership Coaching

Without effective leadership, we are doomed. This is not hyperbole. Without effective and enlightened leadership, the world falls apart—from the smallest community to the most powerful nation and every organization in between. Leadership focuses our intellect and energy. It unites us around common, important goals. It rearranges chaos into order. It is the key ingredient in success.

We know this is true because we see it every day. When wars are being lost, generals get replaced. When a constituency is not happy, politicians get the boot. But companies and organizations need good leaders too. No matter how great a company's product is, no matter how revolutionary its ideas may be, and no matter how impassioned its employees are, without good leadership *the organization will fail.*

Nevertheless, for a long time companies and even leaders themselves were skeptical about the necessity and utility of leadership coaches. "Leadership coaching" sounded too abstract and subjective to spend money on. Some skeptics claimed it was touchy feely mumbo jumbo. They argued that if you had the right monetary incentives in place, it didn't really matter what kind of a leader you were. They believed that the market and individuals' own self-interest would pull the company—and even the entire country—forward. The key, according to them, was to just keep doing what they had always done, only with more efficiency.

However, this simplistic and reductive worldview has been their undoing.

That is because economies grow up. They move from being agrarian to being industrial. Then they even move to a post-industrial stage. What worked perfectly in one economic stage of development doesn't work well in another. Take, for example, leadership style. Authoritarian leadership styles with rigid systems are great for economies made up of primarily basic manufacturing (e.g. China). But they are anathema to economies based on advanced manufacturing and technology (e.g. the United States). One leadership style requires *compliance*. The other gives you *innovation*.

If China and other developing countries want to continue to be successful, they only have to follow the path that developed countries have already blazed. But, in the United States, Japan, and Western Europe things are different. If they are to progress, they will have to head out into uncharted waters—and *lead*. While China can continue to optimize its manufacturing processes, the United States has to find ways to unlock its human capital, so that new things can be imagined, invented, and developed.

What used to motivate people is changing too. A recent PwC report called "Engaging and Empowering Millennials" states the following:

> *Approximately seven years ago, we began to notice a change in the behaviors and desires of our people at PwC. We began to wonder why our younger people didn't seem to be motivated by the same things that motivated the generations before them—why didn't they want to work in the same way? In the accounting and professional services industry, it has long been assumed that fair pay, a stable career path, a chance at financial security, and the prestige of partnership would be enough to attract and retain young talent. However, we started to find that this was no longer the case.[1]*

Corporations are finally seeing the light. They know that their survival depends on leadership that can find and communicate compelling new visions while developing organizations that are agile and committed enough to get there. They know that Millennials need to be communicated with and inspired in a different way than their elders—not only because they make up an increasing proportion of the workforce, but because they are the future.

Investing in leadership coaching is one of the critical means of addressing these challenges. Consider the decisions of a few entities renowned for their "zero b.s." policies, hardheaded scrutiny, analytical intensity, and results-oriented culture: Google, Goldman Sachs, IBM, and GE. According to Forbes, these corporations, along with 25-40 percent of fortune 500 companies, spent more than *one billion dollars* combined in 2012 on executive coaching. IBM alone keeps more than 60 certified coaches on their payroll. Goldman Sachs dedicates tens of thousands of hours to executive coaching. These companies attract the best talent, grow that talent, and then keep it by providing mentors and coaches to their workforce. A survey by PricewaterhouseCoopers found that the mean return on investment (ROI) for companies investing in coaching was *seven times* the initial investment. Twenty-five percent of those companies surveyed reported an ROI of between 10 to 50 times.[2]

Academic research lends credence to these corporate decisions too. A recent paper by two students at Cornell found that there is an increasing shift away from formal education systems towards mentorships (leadership coaching) and that although executive programs—such as special job assignments and international job rotations—are popular, they aren't always the most effective ways of developing talent.[3]

Top business universities, which serve as feeder schools for the country's best corporations, are supporting the executive coaching model as well. The Wharton Business School began an Executive Coaching and Feedback Program in 2012, which is available to all incoming MBA students. The Kellogg School of Management at Northwestern University is also designing, implementing, and facilitating coaching experiences centered on personal leadership development. These experiences compliment the classroom experience in Kellogg's Executive Education Program. These institutions long known for their focus on operational and analytical excellence are finding ways to boost individuals' leadership skills in executive coaching.

In this context, executive coaching can be understood as an *investment* an organization makes to lower the risks of costly failures due to underdeveloped leadership skills. So let's take a

moment to investigate the various ways that
leadership can (and does) fail.

Leadership as a Bottleneck

**An organization cannot be more impactful, more
innovative, or more effective than its leaders.**
Leaders' decisions ripple out from themselves and
spread throughout the entire organization they
lead—to customers, co-workers, suppliers, clients,
and even to the community they are a part of. The
leader's individual actions are amplified for better or
for worse. When leadership fails (or is less than
optimal) the effects can be staggering. This is why
most turnarounds begin with the replacement of the
existing management or the removal of a CEO. It's
a modern day mutiny driven by a crew no longer
willing to bear the cost of the leader's failure.

Lack of Vision

**One of a leader's primary responsibilities is to cast a
compelling vision for his or her organization.** A
leader must use his or her vision as a means of
uniting people around a common goal. An
organization without a vision doesn't know where it
is going, and this means that it can't create or
implement a strategy to arrive at its goals. The

result is a company that operates totally at the mercy of outside forces and luck. Not only is a lack of vision risky for a company's survival, but employees also suffer from a lack of motivation and a sense of purposelessness in their work. Eventually they will either leave the company or begin to look for ways to do as little as possible and still collect a paycheck. Most people want to *go somewhere*. They need to know that someone competent—a good leader—is taking them there.

The cost of a lack of a compelling vision can be difficult to measure because it is often impossible to know "how much better things might have been." Nevertheless, we can attempt to prove the value of a visionary leader by looking at what happens to the stock price of a publicly traded company when a key leader joins or leaves the corporation. For example, after Steve Jobs resigned from his chief executive role at Apple in 2011, the stock immediately dropped three percent. Three percent may not sound like much. But it represents a decrease of about *ten billion dollars* of the company's value. "What did Steve Jobs actually contribute to the company," some might ask, "especially as he had notoriously bad people skills and wasn't much fun to work with." In a sense, that $10 billion represents intangible value that investors attributed to Steve Job's ability to cast a compelling vision that would excite Apple's loyal customers and would inspire Apple's employees.

Squandering Human Capital

Human ingenuity and creativity are limitless. But leaders squander this human capital when they build ineffective teams and foster corporate cultures that are detrimental to the success of an organization. Employees often become disgruntled and unengaged because they are in the wrong place in an organization. The workplace becomes full of dissonance, and productivity and creativity plummet. Turnover skyrockets. Profitability nosedives. Poisonous corporate cultures and caustic teams may be the result of many factors, but none of them is more important than leadership.

Because leadership is such a huge responsibility, it makes sense that executives are increasingly seeking out coaches to help them hone their people skills, to create and cast compelling visions employees can feel good getting behind, and to build teams that people love to work in. The old paradigm has been this: We formally train people how to be engineers and accountants, but not how to be leaders because leadership cannot be taught. Some people get it and some don't. But the new paradigm is this: training someone to be a leader is possible but it isn't about

13

jamming knowledge into the person's head. It is more like training them how to be an athlete; it takes time, discipline, and a sustained effort. Any great athlete needs a great coach, and any great leader needs a coach as well.

What Coaches Do

Perhaps this all sounds a bit too abstract. "What exactly do leadership coaches do?" you may be asking. Fundamentally, a coach helps a client to improve their environment and leadership skills by asking questions and looking for answers.

A Coach Offers a Different Perspective

- Are we looking at an opportunity or a risk?
- Is the employee in question woefully undeveloped or full of potential?
- Is that goal unrealistic?
- Did I handle that situation well?

The answers to these questions depend on your perspective. Leadership coaches and consultants can provide an informed and trained outsider's perspective from which to test assumptions and question judgment calls and, when necessary, to call a client to action. They help clients to strip away some of the bias, confusion, and noise that result from being immersed in an organization so that the client can better see their world as it actually is. This is a way of glimpsing the truth and transforming our experiences and situations so that we are more able to engage with them.

A Coach Finds Out Where You Are, What You Have, and Where You Need to Go

Journeys require preparation. Careful preparation.

- Where are you going and why?
- Do you have what is required to make the journey?
- How will you get there?

Leadership coaches use analytic tools and their keen insight to help their clients find both a personal and corporate vision that fits uniquely with the passions and talents of a particular leader and his or her organization. But it is not sufficient to *know* what you want to achieve. You also need to know *who you are* and if you *have what it takes* to get to where you're going. With a leadership coach, individuals can better determine where the gaps are. Then they can craft strategies to fill or bridge those gaps.

A Coach Helps Determine What Needs to Change

If I didn't believe that people could change and grow, I wouldn't be an executive coach. While it is not a coach's job to "mold" clients, it is often a coach's job to help a client find ways to activate change in himself.

The question is this: In what ways does the client need to change, and in what ways must their environment be transformed for optimal performance? Once this is determined, how can the client and the coach work together to affect those changes?

A Coach Provides Encouragement

If you're a leader, there's a good chance you'll spend some time in the Desert of Doubt—a big lonely place with few landmarks or signs of hope.

You'll know that you are there when you begin asking yourself:

- Am I on the right track?
- Am I cut out for this?
- Will I fail?
- Can I trust my team?

Instead of ignoring these questions, coaches help their clients to face them and address them. Sometimes a successful coaching session is just getting someone back on their feet, and encouraging them enough to help them keep moving and pushing forward.

One of the most powerful ways we keep our clients moving forward is to remind them of all the preparatory work that we did getting them ready for the journey—all the tools we used and effort we put into discovering their personality, strengths, and values, or all the various ways we confirmed that their vision for the future was worth pursuing and that they had the skills and the team to attain it. My clients can always be assured that they did not set out on their journeys in a frivolous or naïve manner. Other times, the best way of encouraging my clients is simply by listening to and helping them process their experiences. It helps when they know that they're not alone. Many leaders really don't have anyone to talk to, and they are worried about the effects of expressing their confusion and anxiety to their employees, their spouse, or their family members.

A Coach Challenges You

- Is this really the best I can do?

- What task am I avoiding?
- How much of the truth can I stomach today?

Growing and getting stronger hurts sometimes. Just ask any athlete. A coach can and should tell you things you don't necessarily want to hear. A good coach will push you to find the limits of your potential.

A Coach Holds You Accountable

- This looks like a great opportunity to make money, but will it bring me closer to my vision?
- Would you call me next week to make sure I've done what I said I would do?
- Am I making progress?

The client and the coach both have to trust and respect each other enough to hold each other accountable to do their best work and stick to the plan.

What Coaching Requires of the Coached

Have you ever noticed how every martial arts movie seems to have a scene in which the protagonist, beaten and defeated, must seek the instruction of a master? What you are less likely to have noticed in these movies is how the master tends to react to the person seeking instruction. The master never unquestioningly offers his instruction or quickly takes in every individual that knocks on his door. Even the place where the master makes his home is remote and uninviting. After climbing a mountain or crossing a desert the individual seeking help finally arrives at the master's door—perhaps only to find that the master seems intent on turning him away. But after the individual demonstrates his perseverance, the master agrees to teach him...if the individual can successfully complete a series of tests.

Why the tests?

The master is trying to verify that his pupil has the *characteristics necessary for success*. If any of the critical characteristics are missing, then there is no point in even taking the first step in training the individual. This selectivity is not the product of arrogance on the part of the master. It is a means of preventing many would-be pupils from wasting their time. Once the master finally accepts the individual as a student, a special bond is formed. From that point forward, if the student fails, then in a sense, so does the master.

I don't claim to be a guru or master. But I do claim to have a system, expertise, experience, and training that can help my clients achieve more with me than without me. I have three requirements for anyone that I coach to become a better leader. My clients must be **honorable, hungry,** and **hone-able.**[4] If they have these three characteristics, I know that they are coachable.

Honorable

"Honorable - Having or showing honesty and good moral character" – Merriam-Webster Dictionary

I said "honorable"—I didn't say "perfect." None of us is perfect. And, thankfully, you don't need to be perfect in order to grow as a leader. In the age we live in, leaders can have many different types of leadership styles, but all of them require that those following the leader do so voluntarily. Coercive, manipulative, deceptive, or fear-based leadership styles do not have longevity, and I wouldn't want to promote them even if they did. I want people to follow you because they respect you for your competency *and* your character. My goal is to be on the side of the good guys. I want to know that if you become better at leading, you will use this skill to make other lives better, not just your own.

Consider the following questions:

- Do you care about doing the right thing?
- Do you care about how you accomplish something as much as what you accomplish?
- Do you care about others?
- Have you made yourself accountable to other people?
- Do you have principles that you try to live by?
- Do you have values that people admire? What have you sacrificed because of those values?
- Are you honorable?

Hungry

Trying to coach someone who does not truly desire to become a better leader is like pushing on a rope. This is why I'm only interested in coaching individuals who are hungry to learn and eager to develop as leaders.

- How much do you think that leadership impacts an organization?
- Are you willing to make sacrifices in order to become a better leader?
- Are you willing to invest time and resources in order to become a more effective leader?
- Are you hungry?

Hone-able

"Hone - To make more acute, intense, or effective" –
Merriam-Webster Dictionary

A leader who is willing to accept healthy criticism makes a humble yet powerful statement to his or her organization. But it is equally important to actually be willing to see and do things differently.

Can old dogs learn new tricks? Are you hone-able?

Part II: Sterling's Approach to Growing Leaders

We begin here. The following are the assumptions on which the Sterling Integrators Leadership Development system is built. We may disagree with clients on many beliefs and ideas, but not on these.

Sterling Integrators's 12 Assumptions

1) Leadership is a big responsibility. People's lives and the world will be changed because of what you do or do not do. For this reason, ethics truly matter.

2) No matter how excellent of a product or service an organization has, without good leadership, it will fail.

3) If you are not convinced that you really can and should develop as a leader, then do not begin the journey.

4) You have to *want* the truth about yourself and your situation more than you *fear* it.

5) Compelling is more powerful (and moral) than coercion.

6) If we don't know what success looks like, we'll never know if we have achieved it.

7) Analysis is only as good as the quality of the data—get good data.

8) Data that doesn't influence you or your organization is useless. Either stop collecting it, or put it to use.

9) Changing your behavior is possible, but it involves pain and hard work. Creating lasting change will require both focus and tenacity.

10) It is important to be conscious of the people and texts you come in contact with because they have the power to change you.

11) Talk more about what you'd *like to be* than what you *don't want to be*.

12) If we don't stick to the plan, we will run in circles.

The Sterling Integrators Leadership Development System (In a Nutshell)

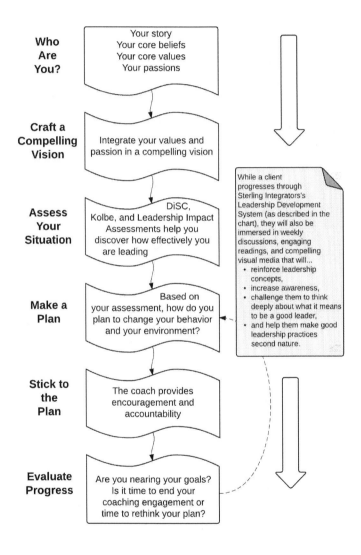

Who Are You?
Your story
Your core beliefs
Your core values
Your passions

Craft a Compelling Vision
Integrate your values and passion in a compelling vision

Assess Your Situation
DiSC, Kolbe, and Leadership Impact Assessments help you discover how effectively you are leading

Make a Plan
Based on your assessment, how do you plan to change your behavior and your environment?

Stick to the Plan
The coach provides encouragement and accountability

Evaluate Progress
Are you nearing your goals? Is it time to end your coaching engagement or time to rethink your plan?

While a client progresses through Sterling Integrators's Leadership Development System (as described in the chart), they will also be immersed in weekly discussions, engaging readings, and compelling visual media that will...
- reinforce leadership concepts,
- increase awareness,
- challenge them to think deeply about what it means to be a good leader,
- and help them make good leadership practices second nature.

The Sterling Integrators Leadership Development System (In More Detail)

Generation after generation has found Miguel de Cervantes's novel *Don Quixote* to be relevant to their lives, but few have sought in it inspiration or ideas about leadership. *Don Quixote* tells the story of a peculiar old man in Spain who, after reading too many books about knights and chivalry, sets out on his own adventure seeking fame and honor as a great knight. The only problem is that he's hundreds of years too late and completely delusional. For over 800 pages Don Quixote, with his pudgy squire Sancho Panza in tow, befuddles those around him, mistaking windmills for giants and prostitutes for royalty.

Neither Don Quixote nor Sancho are examples of exemplary leadership. But their story teaches us something very important about human nature: it teaches us how people change. All the books that Don Quixote read and filled his house with transformed his mind and provided the impetus for him to begin his journey. Long after he had left his books behind, those stories and concepts were still in his mind, and they continued to influence how he saw the world and made his decisions. Also, an astute reader will also notice that Don Quixote and Sancho Panza are not just two people having silly conversations, they are two people with a *relationship* that changes their beliefs and behaviors over the course of their journey.

What we surround ourselves with changes us. Whether they are texts, movies, or people, they will change us. So it is not a matter of *whether or not* we will be influenced, it is rather a question of *who or what* will be doing the influencing.

Because Sterling Integrators believes in the power of relationships, systems, texts, and media to change people, we believe that it is absolutely necessary to use a framework supported by a coherent philosophy to guide leaders in their development. This is very important because without a unified system or philosophical framework, where you end up will be totally unpredictable. A leadership coach without a well-defined idea of what good leadership is along with a proven system for getting there is unmoored. He drifts, and his client drifts with him. Without a framework rooted firmly in reason and well-founded beliefs, a client and his or her coach could easily become like Don Quixote and Sancho Panza, charging together at windmills.

So, on what does the Sterling Integrators Leadership Development System rest? Why should it be trusted?

Sterling Integrators does just that—it *integrates*. Sterling Integrators does not invent proprietary concepts and tools. Instead, the Sterling Integrators Leadership Development System utilizes leadership concepts that work and that resonate with my deepest held beliefs about reality. Both empirically and theoretically, the tools and concepts that constitute the system have been proven to be trustworthy and powerful. Over 40 years of leading teams at companies like Whirlpool, Gentex, and Herman Miller, I have observed what works and what doesn't in the world of leadership. I have identified which environments and types of leadership cause people to thrive. My philosophy on leadership has been heavily inspired by impactful CEOs like Max De Pree and Gary C. Kelly as well as thought leaders like Jim Collins and Daniel Pink.

Biochemists and civil engineers know that the order in which they do something matters. For the biochemist, combining the same substances but in different orders can produce either a lifesaving drug or a deadly poison. Similarly, a civil engineer knows that if she ignores the proper order of operations when solving an equation, it may result in a bridge collapsing. Like biochemists and civil engineers, Sterling Integrators also operates under the assumption that order matters. Growing leaders and strategically transforming organizational cultures requires a process. Although the "ingredients" may change, the order does not.

In the section that follows, I will seek to explain what the steps of the system are and why they exist in the order that they do.

Who Are You and Why Does It Matter?

Superb leaders have a compelling vision. What makes a compelling vision? It begins with knowing who you are.

As the pyramid below illustrates, your life experience shapes your beliefs, your beliefs help to determine what you value, and those values (along with your genetics) will inform what you're passionate about. The top of the pyramid is a vision, which integrates and is alignment with that individual's passions, values, and beliefs. What you are seeking to accomplish or pursue should connect with you on a deep level and fit into the general arch of your story. It should resonate with who you are. At least this is ideally how it should work. For many leaders, their vision does not align with their passion, or is in conflict with their values and beliefs. This kind of dissonance makes leaders irritable, burned out, and ineffective.

It stands to reason then, that gaining self-knowledge will help you to find a vision that is immensely compelling. The problem is that many people fail to realize just how difficult it is to learn about yourself by yourself. Without a rigorous process and the perspectives of other people, deep self-knowledge is impossible. Sterling Integrator's Leadership Development System starts at the base of the pyramid. Like any good structure we need to lay a good foundation and work our way up.

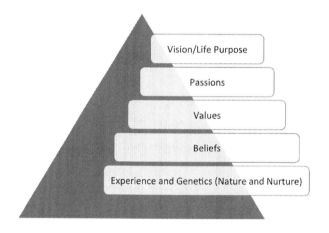

Let's make this a bit more concrete. Imagine that a man named Bill and I, after several weeks of coaching, filled out the following pyramid:

Vision/
Life Purpose:
?

Building things,
Designing things

The group > the individual,
Success = doing something
better than the competiton

Individuals are responsible for using
their gifts and talents,
Indivduals should search for God's will
rather than their own meaning or
purpose

Raised Catholic,
Born in South Africa,
Immigrated to Michigan in 1980,
Strict upbringing with lots of responsibility,
A concrete rather than abstract thinker

Based on the pyramid, which of the two options below will probably make the more compelling life goal/vision for this individual?

A. I want my company to have .5% of the domestic office chair market by 2020.
B. I want my company to receive a design and quality award for one of our products by 2020.

To me, Option B seems to be a better fit. We can see that this individual is more concerned about quality and craftsmanship than with the amount of product that went out the door. Also, something abstract like the gaining of market share would not appeal to them as much as being recognized for something that their organization built and designed.

Our past and who we are does not have to determine our future, but it will influence it. In fact, by understanding what has shaped us and who we are we can take more control of where we want to go and who we want to be in the future. Your vision should be closely connected to what you're passionate about and in alignment with who you are as a person. If your vision fulfills both those requirements, you will be able to pursue it with unshakable conviction.

Your Story

Stories are pervasive in human communities. All cultures and people groups through all of history have engaged in storytelling. Stories are absolutely necessary in order to make sense of the world and our place in it. The stories we tell define us and provide us with meaning. They can empower us or limit us. I have a story. So do you. Each person has a story they tell themselves about themselves, whether they know it or not. Tell yourself a bad story about yourself and chances are you'll live into it. Retell it as a story of hope and possibility and you have provided yourself room to grow and seize a better life.

All this being said, why is it that reading biographies – even those of our greatest historical leaders – can be so boring? The uplifting character arcs that we've come to expect in novels are absent in biographies. And unlike novels, biographies lack the setups created in the first act that are all tied together by the end of the third act, which brings the whole story to a tidy end. Reading a biography can even become tedious at times and it can be unclear how entire decades of the subject's life and various personal trials and tragedies fit meaningfully into the overall story.

While they may not be the easiest genre of books to read, biographies can instruct us and encourage us as leaders in ways that fiction cannot. Seeing how the life of a great leader, such as Abraham Lincoln, is not so different from our own can provide us with valuable perspective and encouragement.

Like many of us, Lincoln was born with few advantages. He was from the backwoods of Kentucky and later claimed that the aggregate of all his formal schooling did not amount to one year. Despite his disadvantages, Lincoln never doubted his intelligence and diligently taught himself every chance he could while working on his father's farm and during a long stint of wandering around Illinois as a young man, trying his hand at everything from owning a store to navigating barges down the Mississippi River. After failure in nearly all his endeavors he became a self-taught (and rather impoverished) lawyer.

His early political career was disjointed and of little note. Far from being on a steady upward trajectory, his path took many detours and plenty of dead ends. His first attempt at running for the state legislature was a failure. On his second attempt he won, but people recognized him more for his immense height and awkward looks than his political prowess. Later he achieved some notoriety as a congressman, but he belonged to the Whig

Party, which was soon to become extinct. After his term as a Representative from Illinois ended, he returned to his law practice for almost a decade, believing that his political career was over. In 1858 he tried for the Senate, but after a long and exhausting campaign against Stephen Douglas, was defeated. Then, much to his surprise and shortly after his defeat, he was nominated by the Republicans to run for President and won.

Even after achieving the presidency, Lincoln's path forward was not certain or clear. He was in over his head and the weight of the great responsibility of unifying a nation weighed heavily upon him. The Union suffered numerous major defeats at the start of the war and many of the people closest to Lincoln began to express doubts about his ability to lead. In his diary, Attorney General Bates noted, "The President is an excellent man, and, in the main wise but he lacks will and purpose, and, I greatly fear, has not the power to command." General McClellan had even greater reservations about his Commander in Chief, stating succinctly in a letter, "The president is an idiot."

Four years later the North and South were reunited, and Lincoln had effectively guided the passage of the 13th Amendment.

Lincoln's life, like many of ours, was full of fits and starts and failures, not gradual and steady progress. We tend to think only of the mythological and grand version of Lincoln and forget about the time he spent drifting down the Mississippi, plodding through another year at his moderately successful law firm, or watching a hard-fought political campaign go up in flames. When we are wandering through uninspiring and difficult phases in our own lives, it would serve us well to remember that real life resembles biographies more than novels and that the last page of our stories has not yet been written.

What's your story?

Your Beliefs

Where are the flying cars we were promised? Are we really supposed to think that the creation of Twitter was a landmark human achievement? Will the future that Star Trek prophesied ever happen? These are the questions that Peter Thiel, the venture capitalist and co-founder of PayPal, is asking a lot these days. He's disappointed with the deceleration of technological and human advancement and he suspects that at its core, this stagnation is being caused by leaders who are ensnared by a very harmful worldview. In other words, their core *beliefs* are holding them back.

After World War II and up until the late 60's, leaders in America were a pretty optimistic bunch. They believed that the world and the future were largely determinate (not to be confused with *deterministic*). According to their view of the world, if humanity could more fully understand the laws that governed the universe and apply imagination to these findings, it could turn an imagined equitable and prosperous future into a reality. These were the decades of the Marshall Plan and the Moonshot – long-term planning, novel ideas, and immense levels of investment. Thiel is nostalgic for an America that was led by artists who envisioned the future and engineers who made it happen.

This way of looking at the world changed in the 1980's when, according to Thiel, Americans began to believe that success had more to do with luck, than imagination and hard work. America's leaders became convinced that the future was indeterminate, completely unknowable and entirely random. When this happened, true innovation and breakthrough ideas dried up. Instead of calculus being the dominate form of mathematics, America became obsessed with statistics and the bell curve's ability to shield those who understood it from risk. Another cultural symptom of this indeterminate worldview was the outsized role that finance, law, and insurance began to play in the economy. Leaders in America no longer created the future, but instead tended the country's legal and financial systems while everyone waited and hoped for the future to arrive. Long-term planning and massive, focused investments were exchanged for incremental change and safe diversified portfolios. America's leaders became observers and managers rather than doers.

Beliefs, these invisible things we hold in our heads, shape our minds and, ultimately, our world. So, we should carefully consider what we believe. While it's easy to let our culture and upbringing hand us all our beliefs about how the world works, critical thinkers like Thiel remind me that the best leaders think for themselves and have the ability to challenge the dominate narrative of society. Is luck more important than smarts and hard work? That is for you to decide, but consider this; how you answer the question will impact your behavior and change the world.

Which of the following quotes do you most resonate with?

"I'm a great believer in luck, and I find the harder I work, the more I have of it."

- Thomas Jefferson

"Success seems to stem as much from context as from personal attributes."

- Malcom Gladwell

Ask yourself:

- What do you believe?
- What do you believe about the world?
- What do you believe about people?
- What do you believe about the origin of the universe?
- What would you consider to be a life well lived?
- Who are you as a human accountable to?

Your Values

Values are your most deeply held convictions about what is important in life. If we were to ask ten people to look at a list of values, pick five of the values that are most important to them, and rank them, chances are, we'd have ten different lists. Leaders who incorporate their values into their work, their goals, and their organizations are creating an environment in which they can flourish and be invigorated. By clearly understanding what it is they value, they can find people who share those values and build a coherent, consistent, and genuine organizational culture. Organizations that are constituted of individuals with shared core values will not be devoid of conflict, but they will have far less of it.

There are two important things to remember before attempting to ascertain your values.

Firstly, the same word can mean different things to different people. As I help clients determine their core values, it's important that we are clear about what we understand each value to mean. For example, the value of autonomy may be thought of as "doing whatever you want" by one person and "freedom to choose how to solve problems" by another. One person might consider a value like conservative to have a negative connotation (unwilling to take risk), while someone else might see it in a more positive light (cautious).

Secondly, it's important to understand that we sometimes mistake our ideals for our values. This can be a hard truth. It is quite a shock when you discover that you are not exactly who you thought you were. When helping a client determine their top values, I begin by asking what they consider to be their core values. Usually it doesn't take long for us to get 5 or 6 values on the whiteboard. That's the easy part. The more challenging part is proving it. Just as we would in a court of law, we'll rely on witnesses, facts, and evidence to seek out the truth.

Once we've created a list of values and agree on how to define them, I ask my clients how those values manifest themselves in their day-to-day lives. We're looking for clear and specific actions that the individual has taken in the past, which support the values she claims to hold.

Here are a few good examples of how someone might complete this exercise:

Integrity	-I make all of our clients aware of the referral agreements that our firm has in place. If any firm that we work with is not comfortable with this policy, we do not work with them.
	- Last quarter I advised a customer against buying one of our machines because I knew that it would be grossly underused and it would be more cost effective to outsource the task they would use it for.
Generosity	-I gave out bonuses last year, even though we did not reach our revenue target, because our low revenue number had more to do with the slow economy than my team's performance.
	- I pay my engineers 10% more than their peers in the industry.
	- I donate 5% of the company's profits to charities.
Community Engagement	- I make a point of hiring individuals from impoverished neighborhoods in our city.
Skepticism	-I do not use a financial advisor. I do my own research when deciding how to invest my retirement savings.
	-My leadership team is comprised only of individuals I have known for five years or more.

Careful introspection with guidance from a leadership coach is useful, but a fresh perspective from outside oneself can deliver the most accurate and least biased perspective of an individual's values. This is why after they've assessed their own values, I ask my clients to have their spouse or family members create a list of values that they associate with my client and then to briefly write about instances that demonstrated those values.

After that, we rank the values, putting the value with the most evidence and support at the top. Many times my clients are surprised to see what was ranked at the top and what ended up at the bottom. Sometimes a value has no evidence at all to support it and so it has to be dropped from the list entirely. It is at that moment that we have discovered an ideal that has been mistaken for a value. Ideals are things you aspire to, but values are lived. Sometimes this can be a bit of a painful realization, but it is necessary to strip away our illusions before we can develop as leaders.

What are your values?
- How do you measure success?
- What will you sacrifice the most for?
- What kind of behavior in others do you find the most irritating?
- Think of a couple of people that you really respect. What do you like about them?

Achievement	Determination	Good Manners	Justice	Persistence
Ambition	Devotion	Gratitude	Kindness	Pioneering
Appreciating Nature	Doing Your Best	Great Music	Laughter	Preparation
Being There	Doing Your Part	Hard Work	Leadership	Purpose
Belief	Drive	Health	Learning	Respect
Caring	Education	Helping Others	Listening	Responsibility
Charity	Encouragement	Honesty	Love	Right Choices
Civility	Equality	Honor	Loyalty	Sacrifice
Compassion	Equity	Hope	Making a Difference	Service
Compliments	Family	Humility	Mentoring	Stewardship
Compromise	Fitness	Imagination	Mindfulness	Teaching by Example
Confidence	Foresight	Inclusion	Opportunity	Vision
Commitment	Forgiveness	Ingenuity	Optimism	Volunteering
Courage	Friendship	Innovation	Passion	
Courtesy	Generosity	Inspiration	Patience	
Dedication	Giving Back	Integrity	Peace	

Know Your Passion

I believe that Dorothy Sayers, the brilliant English writer, captured perfectly how passion and work can be one and the same.

> *"Work is not, primarily, a thing one does to live, but the thing one lives to do. It is, or it should be, the full expression of the worker's faculties,*

the thing in which he finds spiritual, mental
and bodily satisfaction, and the medium in
which he offers himself to God."

A great leader is passionate about her work. Her passion and her work are almost indistinguishable from one another. In order to be passionate about your work, you must be doing something that you are well-equipped to do (think innate abilities and characteristics) and you must be doing something that you believe in (think values). Lastly, you must be working in the way that is optimal or instinctual for you.

There is a terrible misconception emanating from self-help books and life coaches. Perhaps you've heard it. It goes like this: if only you can just determine what you are really passionate about, success will be yours. Many people seem to think that passion is like a hidden river that once you find, you simply have to launch your canoe into and it will carry you briskly away to a land of achievement and success – no paddling required.

As any successful artist can tell you, this is a fantasy. I mention artists because they represent a group of people who accomplish great things by integrating passion with discipline. They have no boards or shareholders to report to. They have few meetings to be at. No quarterly reviews. No one will fire them if they don't show up to work one day, and yet, they keep showing up. Day after day. Consider a few quotes from the greats:

Chuck Close: *"Inspiration is for amateurs – the rest of us just show up and get to work."*

Don DeLillo: *"I've read Borges of course, although not nearly all of it, and I don't know anything about the way he worked – but the photograph [of him] shows us a writer who did not waste time at the window or anywhere else. So I've tried to make him my guide out of lethargy and drift, into the other world of magic, art, and divination."*

Woody Allen: *"So when you're finished with a film, what else do you do? A couple of days go by, you get bored, and I think to myself, let's work. It's how I define my life."*

Andy Warhol: *"Why do people think artists are special? It's just another job."*

My brother, Rick Beerhorst, is an artist working in Grand Rapids and I know that what he does each day depends very little on how particularly inspired or passionate *he feels* that morning. Each painting begins with a vision or a spark and then he spends weeks making daily efforts to work incrementally towards it. He does not require daily inspiration or the presence of a muse. Those are fickle things, not nearly as reliable as practicing a disciplined approach to work and an underlying and undying passion for painting and creativity.

Passion is important. At Sterling Integrators, we consider it the starting point and something that each individual is called to respond to. It indicates in which direction you should be going and provides the initial push towards a new vision. But passion is only half of the equation. So, have the faith to pursue your passion but don't be surprised or distraught when that passion seems to disappear behind the clouds for a while. It will come back and when it does, you should be hard at work continuing on in the same direction as when it left.

What are you passionate about?
- What are you doing when you lose track of time?
- What inspires you?
- What was the most fulfilling task you've ever completed?

Craft a Vision (Where Are We Going?)

I believe that a vision statement needs to be three things.

1. **Bold** – Its attainment is not certain.

2. **Clear** – Visions are specific enough that you know when you've arrived.

3. **Aligned with the People Who Pursue Them** – Visions are in alignment with who you are as a person or a group. As much as possible, they incorporate the values and passions of the people pursuing them.

Here are some great examples of compelling visions:

- **Honda,** in 1970: We will destroy Yamaha.
- **Microsoft**: A personal computer in every home running Microsoft software.
- **Google**: To provide access to the world's information in one click.
- **Ben and Jerry's**: Making the best possible ice cream, in the nicest possible way.

Are you starting to get the picture?

In the early 90's Jeff Bezos had a vision: the internet was going to dramatically change the way people purchased everything and he wanted to participate in that transformation. The idea of Amazon.com hatched shortly thereafter. At the time, Bezos was making very good money at a large hedge fund in New York City. The decision to leave his enviable job and invest every last dime he had into a risky new business venture was not to be taken lightly. Bezos recalls how the decision was much easier to make after he employed the use of what he refers to as a Regret Minimization Framework.

The Regret Minimization Framework is a simple but powerful way to make big decisions. It works like this: Imagine yourself at age 80 looking back at your present situation within the context of your entire life. Of the various decisions you could make today, which one would cause you the least amount of regret when viewed from the perspective of yourself at age 80? When Bezos did this he came to the realization that he might regret quitting his job and attempting to participate in the Internet phenomenon – especially if he failed. However, what would be even more regrettable would be to not try at all.

What makes the Regret Minimization Framework effective is its ability to help you move beyond short-term thinking and the confusion of day-to-day events to a long-term perspective. It's the difference between a rat bumbling its way through a maze and someone using the stars to navigate across the ocean. Bezos left his job halfway through the year, which at a Wall Street firm meant forgoing a big year-end bonus. From the perspective of a person thinking in the short-term, it was stupid, but from the perspective of an 80 year old imagined version of himself, it was the right thing to do. Had Bezos gotten his start even 6 months later than he did, there's a good chance that Amazon.com would not have become what it is today, or even survived at all.

What's really interesting about the Regret Minimization Framework is how not only did it impact Bezos' own life, but it also permeated into the culture and strategic direction of the company that he leads to this day. This was possible because from day one, Bezos knew where he was headed, so he was able to hire only those who "saw" the vision. Amazon.com is well known for the long time horizon of its strategy and growth. The company is perfectly willing to endure quarter after quarter of losses or low profitability in order to achieve its long-term vision. In fact, Bezos' initial business plan did not even project any sort of profitability for the first 5 years of the company. This is refreshing in an age where executives and shareholders are often only thinking about the next quarter's numbers instead of where the company will be a year, or even a decade from now.

Ten years later, Amazon is still here. Many of its competitors are not. It takes an immense amount of resolve to unwaveringly pursue a vision for a decade, but this is the key difference between those who thrive and those who languish. You must be convinced of the validity of what you have set out to do. Your leadership team must be convinced as well. This kind of conviction can only come from careful introspection before one begins creating or looking for a vision. Once that vision is chosen a leader must be disciplined and resolved enough to close off other tempting alternatives and visions so that you can direct all of your resources and time into one coordinated effort. When you resolve to chase your dream, you do not waffle, waiver, or wander; you step out confidently in a predetermined direction. Strategies for reaching your vision can change, the timeline may be modified, the team shuffled, but your conviction that where you are going matters must remain intact. A leader who does not invest sufficiently in introspection will later be dismayed when he finds he is not journeying with a purpose but wandering with frustration instead. I want my clients to know beyond a shadow of a doubt that what they are setting out to do is worth doing and that they are the ones to make it happen.

Take Inventory and Assess Your Situation

Every leader who is pursuing a vision is on a journey. You will be traveling from where you are today to where you want to be in the future and growing along the way. But, as with all journeys, even after deciding where it is you want to go (your vision), there is more work to be done. A couple of more steps of preparation – what we call at Sterling Integrators' "Taking Inventory and Assessing Your

Situation." We need to know where you're at and what you have.

Like a traveler with a backpack full of useful things, you too have things you carry with you that can be either assets or liabilities. They can help you and your organization, or they can hinder. They are: your personality, your instinctual way of solving problems, and your leadership style.

The more you know about these items, the better you'll be able to utilize and leverage them. To learn about your personality, instincts, and leadership style, we'll implement three powerful assessment tools. The DISC Assessment will illuminate how you perceive the world and process information. The Kolbe Index will reveal they way in which you optimally go about getting work done and solving problems. The Leadership Impact Inventory will provide you with feedback about how you're impacting your team and the type of culture your fostering within your organization.

Then there are two things that you won't find in your backpack but are present in the lives of every leader. They are: **Your Achilles Heel** and **Your Saboteur.** Your Achilles Heel is that one great weakness that gets you every time, although you might not be aware that it even exists. Your Saboteur is that negative voice that breeds doubt, fear, and despair.

Before we can better our situations and ourselves, we need to know about them inside and out. What you learn during the Taking Inventory and Assessing Your Situation Phase must lead to changes in both your environment and yourself, but more on that later. First, let's take a closer look at these assessment tools.

Know Your Personality

If you lived in Greece around the year 300 BC, and were a talkative person with a sunny disposition, your friends would probably have described you as being sanguine. Sanguine means blood, which was one of the four bodily fluids (or, humors as they called them), that the ancients believed influenced an individual's thoughts and behaviors. The other three were yellow bile (choleric), phlegm (phlegmatic), and black bile (melancholic). An excess of black bile and you were bound to be a bit melancholy. A deficiency of yellow bile explained why you were shy. Kind of gross and weird, but they were on to something – people do indeed tend to fall into a number of distinct personality categories.

Carl Jung, the highly influential Swiss psychologist, recognized this as well but instead of attributing personality and behaviors to the four humors he attributed them to the subconscious. Jung developed a typology by first categorizing everyone as either being influenced more by the environment around themselves (extrovert) or by thoughts and feelings generated from within themselves (introverts). He went further by suggesting four main categories of behavior. Jung believed that when it came to perceiving the world and taking in information, individuals either prefer the use of senses (utilizing tangible or concrete evidence) or intuition (utilizing abstractions, memories, and patterns.) After this, decisions are then primarily made by thinking (using logic) or feeling (using emotions).

Jung's theory provided the foundation on which modern psychologists and researchers built an array of personality assessments. Their goal being to help individuals more objectively and systematically determine their own predisposed way of being in the world. The most popular of these assessments are the Meyer's-Briggs Test Indicator (MBTI) and the DISC Assessment Profile (DISC).

Sterling Integrators' Leadership Development Program employs the use of DISC rather than MBTI for a number of reasons.

Firstly, while the MBTI helps to illuminate how individuals process information internally, the DISC does a better job of describing someone's behavioral tendencies. In a professional work environment, we don't want clients getting caught up in psychologizing and analyzing each other. This can be a speculative and unhelpful activity, more suitable for a therapist than a CEO. Our focus, and the focus of our clients should be observable behaviors, not the inner workings of the unconscious.

Secondly, the MBTI only describes what your personality will be like in an optimal and stable environment. The DISC Assessment goes beyond that and can predict how your behavior is likely to change in stressful situations, of which there are plenty in most organizations.

Thirdly, DISC is more granular and nuanced than MBTI. An individual who takes the DISC can fall into one of hundreds of categories, while the MBTI boils everyone down into just one of 16 personality types.

DISC Assessment in Nutshell

The four categories that DISC uses to describe human behavior and personality are as follows:

- **Dominance** – Person places emphasis on accomplishing results, the bottom line, and confidence.
- **Influence** – Person places emphasis on influencing or persuading others, openess, and relationships.
- **Steadiness** – Person places emphasis on cooperation, sincerity, and dependability.
- **Conscientiousness** – Person places emphasis on quality and accuracy, expertise, and competency.

After taking the assessment, it is helpful to have a leadership coach to go over the report with you and help you to understand the different behaviors, values, priorities, motivators, and preferred means of communication associated with your personality type. How your personality is likely to change under stress is another concept that should be explored.

Why Is DISC Important for Leadership Development?

DISC is an excellent tool for growing in self-awareness. It can illuminate how you can best contribute to the team, what kind of activities will enable you to be most in resonance, and where your blind spots are. This powerful, perspective-giving tool will also help you to empathize with those who are very different from you, which is absolutely necessary in order to minimize conflict and determine the most effective means to persuade and communicate with the diverse group of people you lead.

Know Your Instincts and How You Work

Michelle was a phenomenal salesperson, so it seemed only logical to promote her to the Director of Sales position. Within three months of her being in that role, the whole department is in disarray and sales are down 15%.

Michelle knows sales and has great emotional intelligence but she's not performing well in her new role. So, what's going on here?

Since the time of Plato, the human mind has been understood to have three main domains or functions: thinking (cognitive), feeling (affective), and doing (conative). The first two have been studied the most and as a result we have many evaluative tools to help us determine what we know and how we feel. Cognitive tests, which assess what you know, include IQ tests, the GRE, the SAT, and industry specific skills assessments. While, affective tests such as the DiSC and Meyers Briggs Type Indicator, focus on revealing your personality, motivation, and values. It is this last function, the conative domain of the mind that has gotten the least attention. This is unfortunate because understanding the conative domain is equally as important as understanding the other two.

Your conative style is how you instinctively respond to a challenge or take action. It is your *modus operandi*. In the 1970's, a sociologist named Kathy Kolbe began studying the conative domain of the mind. Based on information gleaned from a decade spent conducting interviews and case studies, Kathy was able to identify four conative instincts that humans use to problem solve and take action. She went on to develop the Kolbe Index, an evaluative tool, which thousands of individuals and organizations have since used to measure conative instincts.

According to Kathy Kolbe, the four conative instincts are:

- **Fact Finder** – Instinct to learn more, get more information, evaluate, and deliberate
- **Follow Through** – Instinct to organize, develop systems, coordinate, plan, and schedule

- **Quick Start** – To come up with solutions, accept risk, experiment, innovate, and get going
- **Implementor** – Instinct to act physically in the real world, to demonstrate things and use tools

The Kolbe Index is inexpensive to administer and only requires the individual to answer 36 questions, but the knowledge it provides is immensely powerful and oftentimes, immediately applicable. Imagine that Michelle, the salesperson, had taken the Kolbe Index before being moved into her new role as Director of Sales. We might have learned that she had very high Quick Start (gets going, accepts risk, and innovates), which would explain why she was so great at sales, but that her Follow Through (coordinate, planning, attention to details) was nearly non-existent. This knowledge would make us think twice about moving her into a supervisory role. Not only because she might not be good at it, but because she might find the work draining and uninteresting. However, it also might be possible to modify the Director of Sales role so that Michelle could succeed in it. This could be done by allowing her to trade the administrative detail-oriented requirements of the position with someone else (someone with high Follow Through.) Michelle could then take on additional responsibilities she was better suited for, for example, training and coaching the sales team individually.

There is a place for each person to do their best work and make a meaningful contribution, but matching people with positions requires more than just assessing technical aptitude and personality. Conative style is the last critical piece of the puzzle. The closer you stay to who you really are, the more effective and happy you'll be. This is the insight that Kathy Kolbe has provided and it aligns strongly with Sterling Integrators' leadership and organizational development philosophy. We all have instincts, we need to learn what they are and trust them. The Kolbe Index can help us do just that.

Know Your Current Leadership Style

Like ripples radiating out from where a stone has been tossed into the water, your actions impact your direct reports. In turn, they impact their direct reports, and so on down the line until every person in your organization feels, in one way or another, the effects of your behavior and decisions. Everyone agrees that to some degree, individual performance and organizational effectiveness are influenced strongly by the culture and direction set by leadership. But how can we define and measure that impact?

I have found Human Synergistics' *Leadership/Impact*® tool to do just that. This 360-feedback assessment is effective because, unlike other leadership assessment tools, it focuses on how leaders are impacting their teams and the culture they are fostering, instead of making individuals feel that they are being judged as "good" or "bad" people. This allows the individual to see ways that she can improve as a leader without feeling offended or defensive.

Dr. Robert A. Cooke, CEO and Director of Human Synergistics, did extensive empirical studies and found that the way leaders impact their organizations can be broadly categorized into three ways leaders influence others:

1. **Constructive** – A Constructive impact is attained when leaders:
    a. encourage and enable organizational members to approach tasks and interact with others in positive ways that are consistent with personal needs for growth and satisfaction;
    b. reinforce and inspire their subordinates (and others with whom they work) to demonstrate a

balanced concern for people and tasks, focus on the attainment of both personal and organizational goals, and work to reach those goals through cooperative efforts; and, more specifically,

c. promote Achievement-oriented, Self-Actualizing, Humanistic-Encouraging, and Affiliative behaviors throughout the organization.

2. **Passive/Defensive** – A Passive/Defensive impact is created when leaders:

a. compel and/or implicitly require organizational members to interact with one another in self-protective ways;

b. expect and reinforce others around them to prioritize protecting peoples' feelings at the expense of completing tasks (e.g., withhold negative, yet necessary, feedback), subordinate themselves to the organization (follow rules even when they're wrong), and play it safe rather than take reasonable risks that could enhance performance; and

c. promote Approval-oriented, Conventional, Dependent, and

Avoidance behaviors throughout the organization.

3. **Aggressive/Defensive** – An Aggressive/Defensive impact is created when leaders:
    a. drive others to approach tasks in forceful ways to protect their status and security;
    b. reinforce and require their subordinates and peers to emphasize tasks and short-term performance (rather than the interests of people), narrowly pursue their own objectives over those of other members and units, and compete rather than cooperate; and
    c. promote Oppositional, Power-oriented, Competitive, and Perfectionistic behaviors throughout the organization.

Dr. Cooke's studies also suggested that the majority of leaders who've created effective *and* sustainable organizations employ a Constructive leadership style. This all sounds very well and nice until one realizes that having a Constructive impact may not, on the surface, be easily achieved. Cooke believes that it is possible for leaders to develop the strategies that lead to Constructive impact if they work with a coach who will help them employ

Prescriptive rather than Restrictive methods of leadership. Put most simply, Prescriptive means demonstrating and communicating the behavior you want to see in your organization rather than focusing on negative behaviors and Restrictively telling people what they shouldn't do. At Sterling Integrators, we believe that this Prescriptive approach really works, which is why our clients hear more about what good leadership looks like rather than what it doesn't.

People change slowly, and often, very little. *Intentionally* changing yourself is particularly difficult. Read a biography about one of your favorite leaders and you will see how they have certain personality traits and tendencies that manifest themselves at an early age and continue on throughout the individual's entire life. This stubborn persistence of personality and the way it influences leadership style can be frightening to someone who wants to develop leadership skills but feels that their various personality traits prevents them from doing so.

What if the following list were to describe you:

- High level of passivity in personal and professional life
- Spends excessive amounts of time thinking through problems before making a decision

- Tends to make big decisions without consulting others
- Slow to make organizational changes and hesitant to fire underperforming personnel
- Suffers from crippling depression
- Reactive instead of proactive
- Extremely disorganized
- Indirect communication style

Throughout his life, Abraham Lincoln consistently displayed all of those characteristics. Most of these are not the types of characteristics that we would tend to associate with a good leader, and yet, Lincoln's legacy speaks for itself. Lincoln embraced who he was and his personality, which strongly influenced his methods of leadership. By focusing intensely on and developing his greatest strengths – carefully using reason and logic to makes decisions and engineering broad consensus – he was able to compensate for those aspects of his personality that tended to undermine his ability to lead.

In fact, his temperament and personality allowed him to be uniquely fit for the delicate task of emancipating the slaves and reuniting the United States.

The following is an exchange from the movie *Lincoln* (2012). In it, Lincoln, played by Daniel Day Lewis and the radical abolitionist Thaddeus Stevens, played by Tommy Lee Jones are arguing about how to go about leading the reconstruction of the South and implementing the abolition of slavery. The exchange exemplifies Lincoln's reserved and pragmatic leadership style, which enabled him to move vastly different groups of people towards his vision for the country.

> **Thaddeus Stevens:** *When the war ends, I intend to push for full equality, the Negro vote and much more. Congress shall mandate the seizure of every foot of rebel land and every dollar of their property. We'll use their confiscated wealth to establish hundreds of thousands of free Negro farmers, and at their side soldiers armed to occupy and transform the heritage of traitors. We'll build up a land down there of free men and free women and free children. The nation needs to know that we have such plans.*

> **Abraham Lincoln:** *That's the untempered version of reconstruction. It's not... It's not exactly what I intend, but we shall oppose one another in the course of time. Now we're working together, and I'm asking you—*

> **Thaddeus Stevens:** *For patience, I expect.*

> **Abraham Lincoln:** *When the people disagree, bringing them together requires going slow till they're ready to make up—*

Thaddeus Stevens: *I don't give a damn about the people and what they want! This is the face of someone who has fought long and hard for the good of the people without caring much for any of 'em. And I look a lot worse without the wig. The people elected me! To represent them! To lead them! And I lead! You ought to try it.*

Abraham Lincoln: *I admire your zeal, Mr. Stevens, and I have tried to profit from the example of it. But if I'd listened to you, I'd have declared every slave free the minute the first shell struck Fort Sumter; then the border states would've gone over to the Confederacy, the war would've been lost and the Union along with it, and instead of abolishing slavery, as we hope to do in two weeks, we'd be watching helpless as infants as it spread from the American South into South America.*

Thaddeus Stevens: *Oh, how you have longed to say that to me. You claim you trust them— but you know what the people are. You know that the inner compass that should direct the soul toward justice has ossified in white men and women, North and South, unto utter uselessness through tolerating the evil of slavery. White people cannot bear the thought of sharing this country's infinite abundance with Negroes.*

Abraham Lincoln: *A compass, I learnt when I was surveying, it'll point you True North from where you are standing, but it's got no advice about the swamps and deserts and chasms you'll encounter along the way. If in pursuit of your destination you plunge ahead, heedless of obstacles, and achieve nothing more than to sink in a swamp, what's the use of knowing True North?*

There is no one "right" way to lead. And there is no one type of personality that is ideal for leadership. Whether you have a personality more like Abraham Lincoln or Thaddeus Stevens, it doesn't matter. There are strengths and weaknesses associated with both. What matters is that you know who you are. Then, take this self-knowledge and develop a leadership style that works in harmony with the type of person you really are at your core.

Your Saboteur

"You're going to fail."
"You're out of your depth."
"Don't take that risk."
"You're going to screw this up, just like last time."
"You're not smart enough."
"You don't deserve this."

These are the voices of our saboteurs- the distinct voices that rise up out of our subconscious and breed *false* doubts and fears in our minds.

Not all doubt and fear are bad. When they cause us to check impulses and anticipate consequences, they are totally legitimate. Humans have survived for eons thanks to healthy fears that told us to run from big toothy creatures and store enough food for the winter. Healthy fear serves us well today with more modern problems, by compelling us to save for retirement and thinking twice before saying something to a co-worker or superior that we will later regret.

The question is: how do we discern healthy doubts and fears from the lies?

1. **Name the fear:**
   The fear that your saboteur speaks in your ear, like a devil on your shoulder, needs to be recognized and named. Sometimes it is only a whisper that we are barely conscious of, but just enough to keep us from doing what we should do or reaching our full potential. Being aware that we all have saboteurs is half the battle. Once we are aware of them, we can detect them more easily and recognize them for what they are instead of feeling a confusing and vague sense of anxiety or paralyzing fear. When

you hear the voice of your saboteur, listen carefully to exactly what it is telling you to run from and then turn and face that fear.

2. **Whose voice is it?**

   When you hear the voice of the saboteur who does it sound like? An old boss? Your fifth grade math teacher? Your father? More often than not, the voice of your saboteur is that of someone who knowingly or unknowingly said something hurtful to you long ago. It left a deep wound that never really healed. If you can determine who the voice belongs to, it may be possible to determine when the wound was inflicted, and that can help you to predict in which situations you are likely to hear the echoes of that first traumatizing experience and better prepare for it.

3. **Does it generalize?**

   The voice of the saboteur tends to generalize. You always…. You never… Here you go again… This is just like you…
   A generalization implies that things never change and the battle is lost even before it has begun. It suggests that despair is your only option. On the contrary, healthy fears are generally much more ambiguous and complex.

4. **Have you gotten a second opinion?**
    One of the best ways to determine if your
    fears are legitimate or not is to get a second
    opinion. A certified and experienced
    executive coach can really help you by
    offering the perspective of someone removed
    and unbiased enough to help you more
    clearly see reality and to assist you in getting
    to the bottom of your fears or he may refer
    you to another credentialed professional who
    is specialized in the area that you're
    struggling.

It takes great courage and resolve to pick a fight
with your saboteurs and then send them packing,
but you needn't attempt it all on your own. It brings
me great joy as an executive coach to help leaders
silence the voices of the saboteurs that have hobbled
and held them (and their organizations) back for
years.

Your Achilles Heel

For Indiana Jones it was snakes. For Superman it
was kryptonite. For Achilles it was his heel. Every
hero has a weakness and every leader has one too.

This fatal flaw, this weakness is usually the result of either a blind spot or a bias.

- **Bias:** Humans are predisposed to think that their ideas, decisions, and perspectives are the best. We like people who think and act like us. We are biased and our bias is demonstrated by what we choose to focus our time and energy on, who we go to for advice and who we blame when things go wrong.
- **Blind Spots:** We all have blind spots. Blind spots arise out of our unique personalities, life experiences, and educations. What are in those blind spots? Threats and opportunities that we should be aware of but aren't. Things that we can only detect with the aid of someone else's eyes.

How do you know what your Achilles Heel is?

Biases and blind spots can be difficult for a leader to recognize, and for this reason it is imperative that a leader ask for the insight of someone who both knows him well and whom he respects enough to take criticism from. Working together, a leader and this individual can look for patterns of failure. A serious weakness tends to manifest itself in the same way but in different situations over and over. Stamping out the single root of many of our problems can translate into a tremendously improved leadership style and organizational environment. While it is unhelpful to dwell on our weaknesses, it is even worse to be totally oblivious to them.

Analysis and Summary (What Does It All Mean?)

All that you have learned about yourself at this point could fill a book. But, in order for it to actually be useful, you'll need to distill it down to a couple of pages. This is a living document, which means that we can add, delete, and modify its contents as we as we proceed through the Sterling Integrators Leadership Development System.

Your Beliefs:

Your Values:

Your Passions:

Your Vision:

Your Personality:

Your Optimal Way to Work:

Your Leadership Style:

Your Saboteur:

You Achilles Heel:

Make a Plan (How We Will Get There)

You now have a more complete understanding of who you are. You've taken an inventory of your leadership style, your personality and your instinctual way of solving problems. Your saboteur and Achilles Heel have been illuminated. You have a crystal clear vision of where you want to go. What you need next is a plan – a plan for how to get from where you are to where you want to be and where you want your organization to be.

In order to develop as a leader, you must grow and growth means change. But change isn't easy and science sheds some light on why that is. When we repeatedly think or behave in a certain way, permanent connections in our brains begin to form. Over time these connections become deeply engrained neural pathways. When a connection is "hardcoded" into your brain there's no need for it to form new connections every time you think or do something repetitive, because those connections are already there, waiting to transmit a signal. Most of the time, that's a good thing as those established pathways enable you to execute repetitive functions rapidly and with minimal energy and concentration – subconsciously even. If you ever learned a second language, you're familiar with the experience of gradually being able to "think" less when trying to speak in that new language as your brain increasingly translates without you "asking" it to. The more defined and strong those neural pathways, the easier it is to speak in a second language. It's like mental autopilot. And like autopilot it can be a great thing in some instances and in others it can lead to catastrophe.

Sterling Integrators' coaching philosophy and system is informed by this knowledge of neural pathways and the well-known fact that changing behavior takes a tremendous amount of effort.

One of our axioms is that, unless a behavior is completely incompatible with good leadership, we will first try to determine ways to change the environment instead of the individual. Imagine that Sterling Integrators has a client named Frank who is introverted and not very detail oriented but believes that in order to become a better leader he needs to become an extroverted detail person. We could attempt to help Frank change his behavior – but this would probably be a mistake. A better approach may be to help Frank trade or shift various responsibilities that require a lot of extroversion and attention to detail with or to other people in his organization. Unlike intensively trying to help Frank change his personality and work style, changing Frank's environment will solve the problems more rapidly and probably more effectively. At Sterling Integrators, we believe that great leaders come in many different shapes and sizes, so there's no need to hammer everyone into an identical mold.

As much as possible we want our clients to work and interact with other people in a way that is the most natural to them. But, sometimes a behavior cannot be worked around or mitigated and it must be changed. So, given what we know about the challenge of changing one's behavior, what does Sterling Integrators do?

We take a two-pronged approach to behavioral change. The first is what we call a Direct Change Effort and the second is what we call Gravitational Change.

Change Through Direct Effort

By making a concerted effort, applying a lot of energy, and with the help of a leadership coach, an individual really can modify his behavior. Let's imagine that Frank also has an empathy problem. His employees see him as emotionally detached and he keeps irritating those who work for him because he doesn't "get" people. The goal would be to help

Frank actually care about all those people working for him and to imagine how each of them might uniquely see the world. As his coach, I would give Frank an assignment to learn one thing about the life of one of his employees each day by engaging that person in conversation regarding something unrelated to work. Making a resolution to himself is probably not going to be enough to get Frank to follow through with this assignment, so a big part of my job as a coach in such a situation would be to hold Frank accountable and encourage him at our weekly meetings. Technology can help too. Having Frank download an application, such as, Way of Life, onto his iPhone will daily prompt Frank to check a yes or no box depending on whether or not he accomplished his goal. The application will also keep a monthly tally so Frank can see how he's doing. Slowly, but surely, those old neural pathways in Frank's brain will start to disintegrate and new ones will form.

Change Through Gravitational Pull

Anything with mass will exert gravitational pull on objects around it. The bigger the object (the sun, for example) and the closer that it is to another object, the more gravitational force it will exert on that object (the earth, for example). Humans have a tendency to be effected by those around them too, in a sort of gravitational way. We tend to behave like those whom we surround ourselves with. In Frank's case, I would want to bolster the Change Through Direct Effort strategy, by surrounding Frank with individuals (in the form of text, visual media, and discussions) who display the traits he wants to emulate. Then, it's only a matter of time before the subtle Gravitational Pull will accelerate the rerouting of those old neural pathways that keep tripping Frank up.

A good leadership coach will help you to develop a plan for your development as a leader. That is, they will help you to determine:

A. What you need to change about your own behavior *and how*.

B. What you need to change about your environment *and how*.

Evaluate Progress (How Are We Doing?)

People buy invisible things all the time. To prove this, one has only to note the billions of dollars spent each year on education and legal advice. Yet, the buyers of intangibles don't make those purchasing decisions quickly or lightly, and rightfully so. The merits of a car can be judged almost immediately, but the value of an opinion or knowledge may take months or years to be known, and by then, the person who sold it may be long gone. The savvy buyer of intangibles wants proof before they hand over cash. They know that just because something is invisible, doesn't mean it can't be measured. A university can be judged by the percentage of its graduates who go on to be employed in their field of study. An attorney can be judged by the percentage of her clients who have court rulings in their favor, or who don't end up in court at all.

But how do you judge the effectiveness of a leadership coach?

Sterling Integrators' daily work consists of coaching clients, performing analyses, conveying information (derived from analytical tools), and creating strategies, but that's not, ultimately, what we are selling. Clients are paying us to help them become more effective leaders and build more effective organizations. On the face of it, this appears to be incredibly subjective and abstract work. But, if leadership is really as critical as we believe it to be, leadership development should translate into things everyone can witness.

Every six months, Sterling Integrators tracks the progress it is making with its clients by using a combination of the following methods, (depending on what our assignment was):

Personal Experience – Leaders who are leading better should feel better. They should be more engaged, focused, enthusiastic, and resolved. They should feel less stressed out and overwhelmed. Who is better suited to judge the value a leadership coach is adding than the individual being coached?

Financials – Companies that invest in developing above average leaders should have above average profitability because they are able to do more with less and focus on areas where they are uniquely suited to have the biggest impact. Return on equity, net profit margin, sales per employee, and other financial metrics should be positively correlated with money spent on leadership coaching.

Assessment Tools – The Leadership/Impact® Inventory and the Denison Cultural Assessment tools are both utilized by Sterling Integrators to gauge whether or not we're moving the needle on the objectives we and our clients set for ourselves at the beginning of the client engagement. Both of these assessments provide feedback to leadership from whom it matters most – those within the organization.

What we learn from all of this doesn't just disappear down a black hole. We use it to determine, with our client, what is working and what isn't. These findings are then used to make adjustments to our leadership development plan. It is iterative and systematic and it works. We ask a lot of our clients and appreciate the fact that they allow us to hold them accountable. In return, this phase of our Leadership Development System keeps us accountable to our clients. If our clients are not successfully closing in on their goals, we're not successfully closing in on ours.

Part III: Glimpses of Sterling Leadership

A Tale of Two Leaders

It is always a vision that precedes great things. History is full of inventors, entrepreneurs, and artists, all of whom were transfixed by a vision that focused their energies and compelled them to roll up their sleeves and engage in the exhilarating work of creation - transforming an immaterial idea in their brain into something that can be touched, seen, or heard. What they had glimpsed changed them and the world. All of them, when they grew tired and discouraged, were brought back from the edge of despair by what they had seen in their mind's eye, years and sometimes decades before. Their visions pulled them forward and urged them on. So, I'll begin this book by providing you with two visions of leadership – brief glimpses into the fictional lives of Mr. Maul and Larry. They represent the two extremes, the two types of leaders we all have the potential to become. Every choice we make, every belief about the world we choose to hold, and every person we surround ourselves with, will contribute to us becoming either more like Mr. Maul or more like Larry.

Mr. Maul

Heads will roll. Asses will be kicked. If you want something done right, you do it yourself. This is what Mr. Maul is thinking as he hangs up on his Director of Operations and cranks his steering wheel hard to the right, just making it onto exit 66, tires screeching. Tempest Manufacturing, *his* company, looms ahead of him, out of the morning fog. It is a huge facility made out of bricks and steel, invincible looking. But the truth is Tempest Manufacturing is crumbling and on the verge of collapse. Volatile international market forces, the crummy economy, and incompetent employees are destroying it, brick by brick, or so, Mr. Maul believes. Every day is an exhausting race. Can he build up the company more than other forces and people tear it down? He has the sneaking suspicion that today will be no different.

One of the facilities guys is planting flowers near the entrance as Mr. Maul walks quickly towards the main entrance, Matt or Marc, Mr. Maul can never remember which it is.

"Good morning, Mr. Maul," says the man, looking up with a smile.

"Who told you to plant these?"

"Jim Oliver. Said he wanted things looking real nice around here for some big client that's coming here for a visit next week."

Mr. Maul grabbed the handle to the entrance of the building and yanked it hard. "Like we have money for this frivolous crap." he muttered to himself.

Lines one and six were at a standstill. Five men stood around one of the presses. Four of them went scurrying away when they saw Mr. Maul approach, which brought to his mind the image of what cockroaches do when you flick on the lights. Mr. McCombs, Director of Operations was wrestling some twisted piece of sheet metal out of the machine's jaws.

Mr. Maul walked up behind Mr. McCombs with his arms crossed. "Hey, why's line one down?"

Mr. McCombs stopped pulling on the metal long enough to wipe his forehead with the back of his arm. "We shut it down."

"You shut it down."

"You said if Proteous Corp. got behind on payments again, to shut it down and send the workers home."

"I just talked to Proteous this morning. The money's on its way."

"I sent the guys home like half an hour ago, Mr. Maul."

"Do you know how to use a phone?"

"Yeah."

"Well then, use it!"

Wearily, Mr. Maul climbed his stairs to his office on the second floor and shut the door behind him. Glass windows looked out on the production floor. The people and machines down below moved silently behind the glass. He sat down at his desk and started working on a quote for a new customer he had a meeting with next week. It was a long shot, but the potential was huge. Nobody on the sales team was going to touch this. No one was going to screw it up. Two years ago he'd canned his VP of Sales and never replaced him. He had given the guy fair warning, you make your numbers or your gone. He didn't make his numbers. The next quarter, all the sales guys made their numbers.

Someone called and left him a voicemail. He saw the number and felt sick to his stomach. It was the bank again. Usually they waited until the afternoon to ruin his day. Maybe it was all part of a conspiracy to drive him crazy, so they could take his company from him. Others were in on it too. Employees seemed to be whispering more often than usual. Last week he caught two of his top guys talking behind his back (two guys who wouldn't even be getting standard of living raises anymore.) There was a rumor that his head of quality was looking for a new job and recruiters, smelling blood in the water, were going after a couple of Mr. Maul's senior engineers. The production workers, of which they were losing about 5 per month, liked to stay just long enough to get trained before they'd disappear without a word. Customers kept talking about a new company that was edging everybody else out of the market made up of half of the guys who used to work at Tempest Manufacturing. Last week, Mr. Maul had found that his car had a flat tire, a nail he'd somehow picked up in the parking lot. Very suspicious.

There was a soft knock at the door.

"Yeah?" he shouted at the closed door.

It opened slowly and a woman with glasses stuck her head just inside the office. "I'm sorry to bother you Mr. Maul –

"What is it?"

"I just wanted to let you know that I've finished making the adjustments to the cash flow statement like you asked me to."

Mr. Maul kept typing and didn't look up from his computer screen. "Just email it to me."

"Okay."

"And make sure you didn't miscalculate the depreciation like you did last time."

"Okay."

Mr. Maul could sense that she was still at the door. "What?"

You're going to get the roof repaired this year, right.

Yeah. So, what?

Shouldn't we include that expense in the projection that we're sending to the bank?

He stopped typing and looked at her. "Just do what I told you."

"Understood, Mr. Maul," she said and quietly shut the door behind her.

When the money came back he could afford to be nice. When the money came back he could afford to be honest. When the money came back he could stop working 80 hours a week. When the money came back he could get out of survival mode and start thinking strategically again. Now was the time to work harder. Cut more costs. Get people moving!

From a framed picture on his bookshelf his family watched him. Their faces were smiling, but that was three years ago. They didn't smile so much now. The chaos at work had leeched out of the building and infected them all like a disease.

They must have gotten the metal out of the stamping press, Mr. Maul thought, he could feel the thudding rhythm of the machine through the floor. Work harder. Cut more costs. Get people moving. Work harder. Cut more costs. Get people moving.

Larry

Sonya watched an older man through the window stroll up the sidewalk, stop, and inspect the petals of a red tulip and then kneel down to pull out a couple of large weeds. He stood up slowly, shook the dirt from the roots and walked out of her view.

It was the first day of Sonya's internship and her manager, Karen, had invited her to the weekly leadership meeting. Everyone sat in a circle around a table chatting quietly with each other while they waited for the last people to arrive. Karen introduced her to a couple of her colleagues nearby – the Director of Finance, a bearded man named Tony and the Director of Production, Patrice, who wore a bowtie and suspenders. At exactly 8:00, a man on the other side of the table from her stood up and started passing out the agenda for the meeting. When he arrived next to Sonya's chair he reached out to shake her hand.

"Hi," he said. "My name's Dale. You must be our new intern."

"Hi. Yes, I'm Sonya."

"We're glad to have you here, Sonya." He started to continue around the table and then stopped. "I know that boardrooms have a way of making people feel intimated, so I'd ask you to remember that we're all just normal people around here, okay?"

Sonya smiled. "I'll keep that in mind. Thanks."

Dale finished passing out the agendas and went to stand behind his chair. Sonya saw the conference room door behind Dale open and the man from outside, whom she had assumed was a particularly well-dressed groundskeeper slip into the room and take a seat.

"Well, folks," started Dale, "You'll notice that the first item on the agenda is a review of how our quarterly numbers are shaping up. Revenue is in line with what the finance team projected but our gross margin is really starting to suffer. Amy and her team dug into the numbers last week and came to the conclusion that the primary reason for lowered profitability is mostly due to our acquisition of Powder Corp. in October. Increased scrap and some supplier price increases also hurt us, but the acquisition was the key factor, is that correct, guys."

"It is", said Amy, "My team did a great job combing through Powder Corps.' books during the due diligence phase, but we didn't adequately scrutinize the profitability of some of the jobs that the previous owner had already signed contracts for. I am relatively certain that the previous owner of the company bid several of those jobs super low just to ensure that his revenue numbers didn't dip leading up to the closing of the acquisition. Those were pretty big contracts, so we're going to feel the effects of this for at least another quarter."

Someone to the right of Sonya spoke up. "I think we need to confront him about that. We paid a premium for that company and it's obvious that he signed those contracts in bad faith."

A couple of others murmured in agreement.

"There's got to be something in the reps and warrants section of the purchase agreement about that," said Tony, scratching his beard.

"How much of the purchase amount is in escrow?" someone to Sonya's right asked.

The old man who had arrived late to the meeting because he had been sidetracked by tulips leaned forward in his seat. "Patrice, why did we purchase Powder Corp.?"

"Powder Corp. has a unique manufacturing process for the powder coating of MDF board, which we believed that we could more inexpensively acquire than develop internally."

"Do we believe that this is still true?"

"I do."

The old man turned to face someone else.

"Mark, how does the acquisition of Powder Corp. align with our mission?"

"Well, our mission is to build laboratory furniture that we are proud of. Powder coating the MDF board will provide a more durable surface and it's less harmful for the environment. So, yeah, I'd say we can proud of that."

The old man leaned back and spoke to the whole table. "And will the acquisition get us closer to our vision of having our furniture acquired by some of the best research facilities in the world?"

Sonya's manager, Karen spoke up, "Yes, if, and I personally think this is a big if, we can get customers to understand the superiority of powder coating and pay for it."

"True," responded the old man, "And for that reason I want your marketing team to spare no expense to ensure that we roll this out right. Let's have no illusions here. The next couple of quarters are going to be less than stellar from a profitability standpoint. We're going to be spending some real money and we have to be prepared for the fact that there will probably be more costly surprises as we continue to integrate Powder Corp. Bonuses are going to be less than we're used to, but I think that come this time next year we will be very glad we made the investment."

Patrice spoke up, "So, does this mean that we're letting John Allen get away with screwing us over?"

"It does. The money we would spend on legal probably wouldn't justify what we could recoup. Besides, we want Mr. Allen to be a happy camper until his employment agreement expires. He's got a lot of knowledge in that brain of his, so let's make sure we don't make him want to keep it all to himself. Also, Amy, don't beat yourself up over missing those dud contracts. If you'll recall, I'm the one who said that we needed to move fast on this deal. That being said, I'd like for you and your team to figure out how we can minimize the risk of this from happening with future acquisitions. We're probably going to do at least two acquisitions next year."

Amy jotted down some notes. "Will do, I'll let you know what solution we propose to implement by Thursday."

Tony from production leaned forward, "Let's get together after the meeting, Amy, I have some ideas that you might find useful."

"Sounds good. Thanks, Tony."

After the meeting concluded everyone got up and started filing out of the room. The old man stood up and intercepted Sonya and Karen as they headed towards the door.

"I wanted to thank you for your input, Karen," he said. "If there's anything I can do to provide you support from my end, just let me know."

"I appreciate it, Larry."

He turned to Sonya. "Sonya, right?"

"That's right."

How are things going?"

"Really well. This place has such a different feel than the company I interned with last summer."

"Hmm, Interesting. How so?"

"I'm not sure exactly. I guess it's that at the place I worked last summer everyone said all of the right stuff, but I didn't really believe it. They used all of these buzzwords, you know, like teamwork, integrity, and excellence. Actually, I don't think anyone believed it. Everyone here seems really authentic."

"When your internship comes to an end, I'd appreciate it if you'd set up a meeting with me. I want to get your feedback on the 'vibe' you picked up while you were here. Good and bad, unvarnished. Okay?"

"Sure."

The three of them walked out of the room and down the hall together.

"Sonya will be helping us out in the marketing department, but we are going to have her rotate to a couple of different departments to see what kind of work she gravitates towards," said Karen.

"I like the sound of that. Can I offer you a piece of advice, Sonya?"

"Certainly."

"After you're done with all of your rotations, think back to which department you were in when you lost track of time the most. When you lose yourself in your work, you are where you should be. Unless you're losing track of time because you're sleeping."

Sonya laughed "Okay. I'll keep that in mind."

Which Type of Leader Would You Rather Be?

Although few would admit it, many people believe that at its heart, leadership is about getting other people to do what you want them to do. Inherent to this view of leadership is the tendency to see people as tools —objects that are a means to an end, interchangeable and, if substandard, expendable. Leaders within this type of organization constantly use words like: directing, pushing, enforcing, disciplining (sticks), incentivizing (carrots), etc...

True, this is one way to lead. But the costs are high:

- Exhausted and miserable leadership due to the continual pushing and pulling of other people.
- Exhausted and miserable employees who are tired of being pushed and pulled.
- Unengaged employees who seek to extract value instead of add value.
- Cynicism and frustration throughout the organization, which creates a toxic and unpleasant atmosphere.
- A short-term boom and bust cycle, instead of sustainable growth.
- No lasting impact or legacy. If the organization disappears, no one misses it or mourns its departure (some might even dance on its grave.)

Max De Pree, the CEO of Herman Miller from 1980 to 1986, whom I had the pleasure to work under, was one of the key people in my life who helped to transform my understanding of what good leadership looks like. Later in his life, De Pree laid out his philosophy of leadership in his book "Leadership is an Art." In it, he paints a picture of an organization in which individuals and the corporate group as a whole thrive. As the book explains, De Pree's entire worldview sprouted from his deeply held and carefully considered Christian beliefs. If, as Christian doctrine states, each individual is created in the image of God, then each individual is to be engaged with, not exploited or coerced. While contractual relationships have a place in an organization, De Pree valued what he called "covenantal relationships." A covenantal relationship goes beyond rules, transactions, and policies and requires the leader and follower to, have faith in each other, rely on each other, relinquish control to the other in various situations, and, even love one another. Love? An unusual sounding word in the halls of business, some might say. But Herman Miller was never an ordinary company and neither is any organization with exceptional leadership.

Instead of seeing humans as containers of energy and skills to be harnessed like a team of horses, De Pree saw each unique individual as a plant in a garden to be nourished and protected, so that it could grow to its full potential. Only then could the organization as a whole reach its potential. Instead of coercion or deception, the leadership at Herman Miller compelled employees to contribute to a cause greater than themselves and work towards a vision that they all had a stake in reaching.

Here are a few examples to illustrate the environment De Pree cultivated at Herman Miller:

- Employees were freed from their fears of speaking up or making mistakes.
- Whichever employee within the organization was best equipped to understand a problem had the authority to solve it (and was financially rewarded for doing so.)
- Artistic and creative people were not only valued, but were given tremendous freedom to explore their ideas and concepts.
- Managers could incur short-term losses in order to achieve long-term results.
- Anyone who worked for more than a year received Herman Miller stock and became an owner.
- How an employee did something was as important as what he or she accomplished.

You may be tempted to think that these are just pretty words and that in the "real world" or tough economic times this type of leadership philosophy is pure b.s., but I worked at Herman Miller in the 80's and I can tell you that De Pree *actually* believed what he said he believed and *actually* put those beliefs into practice and those practices *actually* created an environment that generated furniture that sits in modern art museums all over the world. The company made a good deal of money as well. I can also attest to the number of lives (mine included) that were changed for the better and given meaning by working at, of all things, a furniture factory!

Then again, this is mostly my own anecdotal experience. Perhaps the more skeptical among you would like some cold hard empirical evidence. We turn now to what has become in the business world nearly a sacred text, Jim Collins' *Good to Great*. In his book *Good to Great*, Jim Collins describes his attempt to understand what caused good companies to transform themselves into great companies.

As Jim Collins explains:

"My research team and I completed a five-year project to determine what it takes to change a good company into a great one. We systematically scoured a list of 1,435 established companies to find every extraordinary case that made a leap from no-better-than-average results to great results. How great? After the leap, a company had to generate cumulative stock returns that exceeded the general stock market by at least three times over 15 years – and it had to be a leap independent of its industry. In fact, the 11 good-to-great companies that we found averaged returns 6.9 times greater than the market's – more than

twice the performance rate of General Electric under the legendary Jack Welch."

Collins goes on to explain the key requirements and underlying variables that his research team and he uncovered that are required for turning a good company into a great one – many of which I'm sure you are familiar with including the flywheel concept, hedgehog principle, and getting the right people in the right seats of the bus.[5] But the most surprising factor, according to him, was the type of leadership that turns a good company into a great one. He calls it a Level 5 Leader, which is a leader who is deeply passionate, committed, humble, and thoughtful. In other words, it was exactly the kind of leader that I found Max De Pree to be and a far cry from the swaggering, charismatic, cigar-chomping ass kicker that many people erroneously believe they must become in order to "get things done."

The Traits of a Sterling Leader

My hope is that you have caught a glimpse of two types of leaders that it is possible to become and that I've made a compelling case for why you should strive to become a leader more like Larry and Max De Pree than Mr. Maul. In the next section of this book, I will attempt to briefly describe 20 traits that, if you are able to attain and strengthen, will enable you to grow into the type of leader that makes a company not just good but great. This next section also serves as a dictionary of sorts. Words are tricky things and the same word can mean very different things to different people. For this reason, it is important that we define our terms and words. I want to be sure that when I use a sometimes ambiguous word like, "humility", "ethical", "sustainability", or "culture", that we both mean the same thing.

Sterling Leadership Trait #1: Lives By an Ethic or Moral Code

Effective leadership is a lever and the individual who wields it possesses a great deal of power. Their efforts are amplified because what they say and do impacts not only those within their leadership team and their organization, but their community. The mobilization of people and resources under the direction of leadership can be an astounding force of good or evil, depending on who is in charge. Effective leadership enables honorable people to do great good in the world and dishonorable people to do great evil. For this reason, I am interested in working with people who know that following the law and responding to the market are not adequate for guiding all of your decisions. At Sterling Integrators, we believe that it is not enough to be an effective leader, you must be a good leader. If you attain all of the other 19 traits except for this one, you and I may end up doing more harm than good.

Perhaps a brief story will help to illustrate my point. In 2004 business was good for Goldman Sachs and getting even better. The financial giant had recently devised a new way to make money by bundling sub-prime mortgages into securities (what they called Abacus bonds), peddling the shoddy securities off to pension funds, and then helping other clients to bet against the same shoddy securities they had just sold. Goldman employees seemed to be fully cognizant of their unethical behavior and quite pleased with themselves, as we can surmise from the internal emails they sent to each other, such as the following:

> *"Just made it to the country of your favorite clients [Belgians]!!! I've managed to sell a few abacus bonds to widows and orphans that I ran into at the airport..."*

In late 2008, when the worldwide economy was in freefall (in large part due to the financial industries' malfeasance), Goldman's scheme came to light and was met with public outcry. People demanded justice, especially since it was they, the public, that were now paying for the massive bank bailouts that were keeping the financial system afloat. Oddly enough, six years later not a single high-level financier has gone to jail or been stripped of their ill-gotten gains. The reason? While Goldman Sachs and other financial institutions had engaged in unethical behavior, they hadn't broken any criminal laws (thanks to the financial industries diligent army of lobbyists) and all lawsuits were being settled out of court. No one was fired and leadership was never held accountable.

What does this mean?

It is possible to make a fortune while destroying the world, and it does not require breaking any laws to do so. So, it's not simply a matter of looking to the law (governments) or markets (economics) to tell us what is right and what is wrong. Governments overlook injustices on a regular basis and markets will happily facilitate the buying and selling of junk. These are human institutions, which mean that they are as corruptible and fallible as the humans that comprise them. They are far too frail and faulty to be used as moral and ethical guide rails.

The story of Goldman Sachs also teaches us that an organization cannot be more ethical, honorable, or good than the people leading it. It starts at the top and ultimately leadership is responsible for the impact that their organizations have on the world. This then implies that our only hope for building good organizations is to pursue good ourselves. We must then submit ourselves to an ethic or moral code that transcends individuals, governments, laws, nations, markets, traditions, and culture. It seems to me that this can only be God and/or reason. Ultimately, every ethical or moral framework rests on God, reason, or a mystical combination of the two. If you have an ethical or moral framework, now would be the time to inspect it closely and if you don't, now would be the time to find one.

So then, how should one live? How do we determine what the right thing to do is? Many of us have a vague idea or loose framework we use to think about these things but would benefit from thinking about them more rigorously and hearing from different voices throughout the world and history. We have a long list of philosophers, thinkers, and religious leaders to look to. All of them asked these same questions and attempted to answer them. One such figure, who contributed massively to this discussion, was our 2,000 year old Greek friend, Aristotle. In Book II of the Nicomachean Ethics he said:

> *"Anyone can become angry. That is easy. But to be angry with the right person, to the right*

degree, at the right time, for the right purpose
and in the right way – that is not easy."

In the quote above, Aristotle is essentially talking about balance – or, in his words, finding the golden mean. The golden mean is a moral virtue that resides between two extremes (vices). For example, courage is a virtue that lies between cowardice (too little confidence) and rashness (too much confidence). It is important to note that Aristotle is not saying that the golden mean of, say, courage is always located at the same place in between the two extremes. The ideal place to be between cowardice and rashness would differ depending on the situation.

For example, let's say that you're trying to find the golden mean of modesty, which you know resides somewhere between shamelessness (too little shame) and bashfulness (too much shame.) The optimal behavior and mindset for you will be different depending on whether you're going to an employee's birthday party or a ceremony thrown in your honor to receive a lifetime achievement award. Not showing up to receive a lifetime achievement award would be to error on the side of bashfulness, and going to an employee's birthday party and dominating the conversation talking about your own accomplishments would be to error on the side of shamelessness. When attending the birthday party the golden mean would be closer to bashfulness, when accepting your prize, the golden mean would be closer to shamelessness.

The table below illustrates this concept further:

Too Little	Virtue	Too Much
Stinginess	Generosity	Extravagance
Sloth	Ambition	Greed
Secrecy	Honesty	Loquacity
Quarrelsomeness	Friendship	Flattery
Self-indulgence	Temperance	Insensibility
Apathy	Composure	Irritability
Indecisiveness	Self-control	Impulsiveness
Cowardice	Courage	Rashness

This is by no means a complete framework for making decisions in our lives, but it is a great starting point for thinking more deeply about what is right and good. Over time we can improve and solidify our own ethical and moral framework. The next step is even more challenging. We have to submit ourselves to the moral/ethical framework we have chosen. And we have to stick to it—at home, at the office, and elsewhere. We need to communicate how we distinguish right from wrong and let others hold us accountable. If we pick up these frameworks when they are convenient and set them down when they are not, we have not truly committed to them, and they serve no real purpose.

We are shaping them, they are not shaping us or our organizations.

And it is in this way that individuals and organizations go about the tragic business of losing their souls.

Sterling Leadership Trait #2: Has Humility

Without true humility, you cannot become or be a great leader. If you don't agree, it might be because you misunderstand what the word means. Humility is not weakness. Nor does being humble mean thinking that you are insignificant, worthless, or that you must deny your own accomplishments. Nor is it about maintaining a false sense of modesty. Humility is about reducing your own self-importance so that you can grow and so that something bigger than you can be created.

I have noticed that the higher someone climbs in an organization, the less likely he is to have someone else alert him to the fact that he has a piece of spinach stuck between his teeth. We all understand why no one wants to be the bearer of this unfortunate news, but why after someone finally brings it to their boss' attention does the boss get a little bit irritated and secretly wish that everyone had just pretended nothing about his appearance was amiss? I would argue that it has everything to do with humility. The spinach example illustrates that humility does not come easy because it requires admitting to our own ignorance and imperfections. This admission damages the perfect façade we want to project to the world.

Why is humility such a difficult virtue to develop? In short, it's because of human nature. First of all, humans like feeling good about themselves. When someone tells us something unflattering about ourselves or exposes our fallibility or ignorance, it deflates our ego. Secondly, humans, from cradle to grave tend to believe that the world revolves around them. Or, put another way, each person sees themselves as the lead star of their own play. All those other people that he or she interacts with every day are just supporting actors. However, people with a good dose of humility, understand that life is actually a play with many characters, of which, they are but one. Instead of being the perfect star of our own play, we need to see how the part we imperfectly play fits into the overall story. Why?

A leader should desire humility for three key reasons:

1. Humility keeps you from becoming the type of person whom you would hate to become

– namely, a jerk or a pompous ass. Humility is about acknowledging the intrinsic value in every person, no matter their job title or background, and elevating them to your level. Humility requires a change of perspective that reduces the gap between how much you value yourself and how much you value others.

2. Everyone has had an experience when they were totally convinced about one thing or the other only to later discover that they were completely wrong. It pays to remember such things. Humility enables you to be open to the truth and accept it as it arrives to you whatever the situation or the person who brings it. We need to have humility about who we are and what we know. Humility allows you to learn new things and admit it when there is a better way than the one you've chosen. Max De Pree wrote several short but great books on leadership, and what strikes me about these books is how little he talks about himself in a self-aggrandizing way. The books consist mostly of what Max has learned from others whom he admires. They are honest accounts of how he used to think one way, learned that he was wrong and now tries to think and behave differently. While he could stand in

the spotlight and talk about his many accomplishments, he chooses instead to highlight those around him and how much they helped him to develop his skills.

3. Humility allows you to accomplish something greater than yourself. If it's only about you, it will never be bigger than you. Humility is also about backing away from the limelight so that others can be seen, heard, and make a contribution. Jim Collins described this concept perfectly in an interview with Fast Company:

   Fast Company: *The CEOs who took their companies from good to great were largely anonymous. Is that an accident?*

   Jim Collins: *There is a direct relationship between the absence of celebrity and the presence of good-to-great results. Why? First, when you have a celebrity, the company turns into "the one genius with 1,000 helpers." It creates a sense that the whole thing is really about the CEO. At a deeper level, we found that for leaders to make something great, their ambition has to be for the greatness of the work and the company, rather than for themselves. That doesn't mean that they don't have an ego. It means that at each decision point—at each of the critical junctures when Choice A would favor their ego* *and Choice B would favor the company and the work—time and again the good-to-great leaders pick Choice B. Celebrity CEOs, at those same decision points, are more likely to favor self and ego over company and work.*

From my positive experience at Herman Miller working while Max De Pree was at the helm and based on Jim Collins' empirical research, I believe that humility truly is the secret ingredient that allows leaders to grow, doggedly pursue something larger than themselves, stay keenly in touch with reality, and gain the respect and loyalty of their employees.

Sterling Leadership Trait #3: Seeks Self-Knowledge

Have you ever made someone really, really angry and had no idea why? Have you ever felt directionless and unmotivated? Are you constantly stressed out? Have you ever gotten what you thought you wanted and it left you feeling unfulfilled? Have you ever felt like you were running in circles? Do you make the same mistakes over and over again no matter how hard you try not to?

Many of these struggles and problems would not exist if we knew ourselves better. Leaders can't be effective if they don't know what they want, don't know where they're going, and don't know what is holding them back. Even thoughtful and self-reflective people struggle to answer these questions. Without a structured method for introspection, proven assessment tools, and the perspectives of people other than yourself, your own self-knowledge will be, at best, limited and incomplete.

At Sterling Integrators, we have been inspired by the process the Society of Jesus (or, Jesuits, as they are more commonly known) use to answer these same questions. A 16th century Spaniard named Ignatius of Loyola founded the Jesuits with the intent of building an elite and loyal group of mission minded priests. Knowing that the path of priesthood was long and at times exceedingly difficult, Loyola wanted to select candidates who would make their vows with absolute resolve. He believed that only through a long and rigorous period of self-discovery, like he himself had gone through, would someone be capable of making such a major commitment. Today, the process of becoming a Jesuit still reflects Loyola's emphasis on self-discovery and careful decision-making. All Jesuit candidates must spend two years of intense introspection and discernment in the form of silence, reflection, prayer, study, discussions with mentors, pilgrimaging, and serving the most marginalized people in society. Through these experiences the novice begins to answer the questions, "why am I doing this?" and "can I achieve the goal that I am pursuing?" By the end of the two years, the novice will know whether or not he has the resolve to take the final vows of poverty, chastity, and obedience.

Sterling Integrators does not ask its clients to go on a pilgrimage or live silently in a cave for months, but it does require its clients to go through a process of self-discovery. We believe that the best way for our clients to discover the core of who they are and what they are about is through engaging discussions, grappling with texts, the use of evaluation tools, and disciplined reflection – all within the context of a leadership coaching environment. By these means, we seek to help our clients to answer the following questions about themselves:

- What do I most value?
- What do I most desire?
- What is the best way I could spend my time?
- What are my alternatives?
- What am I willing to sacrifice?
- What are my core competencies?
- What are my weaknesses and can I minimize and work around them?

When the answers to these questions are in alignment with or supportive of your vision for the future, you will have the resolve necessary to move forward.

Sterling Leadership Trait #4: Understands the Power of Mimesis

Every once in a great while, a unique thinker develops a theory, which if correctly understood, can change the way we see the world. Like a lens, a theory brings things into view that before we could not see and reveals order where once we saw only chaos. It is the knowledge that the theory reveals which enables us to change our world – for better or worse. Take Einstein's theory of relativity, for example. While the theory began simply as one man's hypothesis of reality, before the century was out, the knowledge it had unlocked had helped to both power cities and level them.

A theory does not have to reveal a physical law in order to be earthshaking. Recently, I have become aware of Rene Girard, a French-born, American academic, who for the last 40 years has been developing a theory about human behavior. Like all great theories, Girard's has important implications for many disciplines and fields of human knowledge, including leadership and organizational development. Put most succinctly, Girard's theory is this:

- We want what others want. Humans learn what to desire by watching what others desire and then desiring those same things. Girard calls this mimesis or mimicking and it challenges the predominate belief that humans' desires arise spontaneously from within themselves.
- If we learn to desire what those around us desire, then this means that we will all tend to desire the same objects (people, things, ideas). When there is not enough of these newly desired objects for everyone to have, those objects will be fought over. Girard believes that this is the source of most human conflict and violence.
- In order to resolve this conflict, humans find a scapegoat, blame everything on it, and "sacrifice" it. The destruction of the scapegoat then temporarily returns peace to the community. Girard believes that evidence of this can be found in nearly all human history and mythology. In ancient times, it was frequently an animal or individual that would take the blame (undeservedly) and was sacrificed. In modern times, the scapegoat has all too often been ethnic and religious minorities who have been blamed with no real justification and then "sacrificed".

Interesting theory, but what does it have to do with leadership and organizational development? The following are three applications of Girard's theory for those leading and working within organizations to consider:

Follow the Leader

Organizations tend to reflect the values and "spirit" of those who lead them. Girard's theory explains why this is. The CEO, whether she knows it or not, is daily demonstrating/communicating what she desires. Those who report to her, whether they know it or not, mimic her desires and the desires of those around them. This mimicry cascades down throughout the organization. If the leader desires self-actualization, high ethical standards, excellence, and serving the customer, then chances are, so will the rest of the organization. If the leader desires power, glory, and prestige, then chances are, so will the rest of the organization. The incredible influence leadership has on the organization is why it is exceedingly difficult for organizations to change through grassroots or middle management efforts. If leadership is not onboard in an effort to transform the culture of an organization, change cannot suffuse the entire organization. On the plus side, it really is possible to radically (and relatively quickly) transform an organization, if leadership is itself radically transformed.

The Root of the Conflict

Girard's theory also helps us to recognize what is at the root of most conflicts that are present in organizations. When everyone desires the same *scarce* things, (prestigious positions, huge sums of money, or the sole recognition for an accomplishment), conflict is sure to follow. The solution is to create organizations in which the desired objects are not scarce. For example, serving the customer, contributing to the team, improving a product, or mastering a skill. These are all infinite objects and if leadership can learn to desire them, then so can everyone else. The pursuit of these infinite objects can then bring people together, rather than the scarce objects that tear them apart.

Searching for Scapegoats

Everyone knows that a scapegoat is never the root of the problem, but few people recognize when they are attempting to turn someone else into a scapegoat. Any time that we accuse *one* person in our organization for all of its dysfunction, or one customer for our bad quarter, or one department for missing our numbers, we have probably created a scapegoat. Creating a scapegoat oversimplifies a problem and isolates the accuser from any responsibility. Instead of getting to the root of the problem, it is buried.

Girard's theory began to take shape only after he had spent years reading literature and studying history. He saw patterns emerge throughout all of human history and across cultures. Aspects of human nature that were impossible for one person or people group to see in themselves became obvious when someone could back up and get the perspective required to see the whole picture. As a diligent student of human nature, Girard was able to uncover the hidden forces that impact our behavior. As leaders, we will benefit greatly if we too can understand the forces that Girard revealed, so that we can both harness them and avoid the conflicts they can produce.

Sterling Leadership Trait #5: Is in Resonance

Jiro Ono is in resonance when he's making sushi. I know that he is in resonance because Jiro Ono doesn't just make sushi, he dreams of making sushi. The 89 year-old Japanese man has been perfecting the art of sushi since he was nine years old and despite being declared a national treasure by Japan, he still believes he has not yet reached the pinnacle of his craft. He has no plans for retirement and claims to dislike national holidays because it means he can't go to work. Did I mention that in his dreams he has visions of sushi?

When an individual is in resonance, it means that they are doing work that engages them on a deep level and they are performing that work in the way that comes most natural to them. By this definition, Jiro Ono is most definitely in resonance. Are you?

You know you are in resonance when:

- You lose track of time.
- You go home and you think of the solution that has been eluding you all day.
- You struggle, but you want to keep working at it.
- Your work is not a means to an end, it is the end.
- You seem a bit crazy to those who don't know you.
- You are thinking mostly about the present, not the future or the past.
- You don't regret how you have spent your day.

- You feel a satisfied kind of tiredness at the end of the day.

In order to be in resonance, you must love your work. In order to love your work you must be doing something that you are well-equipped to do (think innate abilities and characteristics) and you must be doing something that you believe in (think values).

A great leader must love their work. Before I go on, I'd like to make a couple of points clear about what loving your work doesn't mean:

- Loving your work does not mean that it will always be effortless and fun but it does mean that it will be engaging and fulfilling. A professional athlete goes through a lot of pain in order to play well a championship game.
- Loving your work does not mean that you must live an unbalanced life and make those around you suffer. If you'll recall in Moby Dick, Captain Ahab did not love his work, he was obsessed by it – and ultimately, destroyed by it via a very unhappy whale.

But there's something else that is required in order for a person to be in resonance; they must be performing the work they are passionate about in a way that comes naturally to them and in an environment in which they thrive. We all have our own instinctual ways of approaching work and solving problems and we have environments that we prefer over others. Someone who is extremely organized and feels that thorough research is necessary before making decisions will have a much different optimal way or working and environment in which to do that work than someone who is more impulsive and enjoys being in the middle of all the action.

Sometimes only a slight adjustment is necessary for someone to achieve real resonance. Other times it requires a seismic shift.

Sterling Leadership Trait #6: Knows How to Create a Team

You build a great team by finding and hiring the best, smartest, and hardest-working individuals and putting them in the right place within your organization. If only it were that easy. While I find Jim Collins' "get the right people in the right seats of the bus" metaphor logical, I also find it a gross simplification of how great teams are actually formed and developed in the real world. A better metaphor would probably be, "you've crashed your airplane in the desert and now you'll have to find a way to get the survivors to work together to get home." Most of the time, leaders find that they must work with the team that you have, not the "ideal" team that they can imagine. This is because in the real world we operate within constraints. There are limited budgets, disappointingly small pools of candidates, an abundance of average employees, and more than a few long-timers who, for various reasons, are more risky to try to let go than to keep around.

The bus metaphor also obscures the fact that qualifications and credentials are only half the story when it comes to building a team. Real teams are comprised of individuals with different values, quirks, and preferences who interact continually with other individuals who have their own different values, quirks, and preferences. This plurality and diversity of personalities is a double edged sword that both makes organizations strong and dynamic, while at the same time being a potential source of conflict and division. The effectiveness of a team is not only improved by optimizing the configuration and tweaking the employee roster, but by improving the emotional intelligence of the whole group. People who understand themselves and others are more likely to proactively solve their own conflicts and be aware of who they need to work with to mitigate their own weaknesses. The next step is to create an environment where a true team mentality can be forged.

If you want to see how a real team is built and developed, I would recommend watching the HBO television series The Wire. When The Wire was aired in 2002 critics and viewers alike lauded it as a phenomenal work of popular culture. Its portrayal of Baltimore revealed the complex web of drugs, crime, police, bureaucrats, and politicians that have caused the city to be mired in poverty and violence. Much less talked about, but equally intriguing to me is how The Wire illustrates leadership and teamwork. The series begins with the formation of a special police unit that is tasked with taking down the Barksdale Crew – a powerful and growing criminal organization in West Baltimore. It soon becomes clear to Cedric Daniels, the narcotics lieutenant in charge of the special unit, that the police chief doesn't really want them to be successful; he just needs to appear to be taking action to appease those in even higher authority. For this reason and because the department is nearly broke, the special unit is comprised of mostly subpar police officers and is forced to literally operate out of a dingy basement. Lieutenant Daniels is up against a sophisticated enemy, is being hamstrung by his own boss, and his team is comprised primarily of alcoholics, guys two years from getting their pensions, and other people that various departments have been trying to get rid of for years. Over the course of the first season, the team is transformed from a clunky and dysfunctional group of misfits to a highly effective crime fighting team that begins to bring down criminal bosses and crooked politicians alike. This transformation does not happen by blind luck or magic, but by a conscious effort of Cedric Daniels and the more senior members of the team.

As The Wire suggests, true teamwork is something that appears and grows when the right conditions are present, it is not simply just a matter of who is on the team. The recipe for creating those conditions is not overly complex, but it's no simple task either. You'll need to shift the people you have into roles where they can do their best work and break up cliques that are comfortable with each other but not productive. Find out who is operating far beneath their potential and what gaps they can fill. Communicate a clear vision of where you want to take the organization and make it compelling enough so that people want to go there too. Those who are not interested must part ways sooner rather than later. Tasks and objectives must be structured in such a way that team work is actually possible, and you'll need to provide the trust and freedom necessary for people to naturally gravitate towards each other and solve problems as they see fit. Get the compensation structure right, so that people are incentivized to think and work as a team, and provide them with the resources necessary to do the job right. Step in when necessary to resolve a conflict but not before the team has had an opportunity to resolve the issue themselves. Do these things and you'll find that building and growing an effective team is not dependent on recruiting exclusively from Ivy League schools or spending tens of thousands of dollars on corporate team building activities.

Sterling Leadership Trait #7: Is Committed to Growing Their People

Many leaders of organizations behave like a ship captain who insists on (or actually has to be) involved with every task on the vessel – raising and lowering the sails, dropping the anchor, making the navigational calculations, coiling the ropes, etc.

By being involved in all of the operations necessary to sail a ship, that same captain is putting the entire enterprise at risk for two reasons:

1. He's not keeping an eye on the horizon or his maps (risks: falling off course, missing out on opportunities, and failing to see danger)

2. He's not making sure that the crew is satisfied and engaged (risks: desertion and mutiny)

I have found this to be an incredibly prevalent problem throughout my professional career, especially within small businesses. The solution would seem to be simple: delegate tasks and responsibilities. And yet, this isn't happening. Why?

Most leaders would say it's because they lack a sufficient number of "crewmembers" with the competence to handle the really important stuff and they don't have the funds available to hire more.

Developing internal talent solves both of the problems listed above. Unfortunately, the way that many leaders 'develop' those within their organizations tends to be very hands-off and demoralizing. I would describe it as a process of observing who the most ambitious and politically inclined employees are and then letting those people duke it out to see who can earn a place of more power and prestige. All too often, growing professionally is seen as something only a small percentage of the entire organization is really capable of and it is up to those individuals to self-identify and maneuver themselves into their new roles. In such a scenario, all leadership can do is observe, and when the time is right give out promotions. The message is clear: only the minimum will be required of most employees and those who know how to work the system will get ahead. Is it any wonder why so many leaders complain about being overly busy due to a chronic shortage of truly capable people to whom they can delegate important tasks?

The solution is to actually develop talent instead of waiting for it to emerge, which requires a belief that everyone has potential they are not fully actualizing *and that they themselves may not even be aware of*. A turning point in my own life was the result of people seeing more in me than I, at the time, saw in myself. When I was 16 years old my father, who noticed that I loved tinkering with electronics and taking things apart, informed me that I would be working for a certain Bill Paberzs who owned a service station near our house. Bill recognized both my aptitude for mechanical things and saw my potential, despite my near complete ignorance of automotive diagnostics and repair. For years he invested time and resources into my development. Bill was literally a hands-on teacher – he would put his hands on mine to show me how to correctly use a torque wrench. With great intentionality, just the right amount of instruction, encouragement, and constructive criticism, he helped me transform myself from someone who could barely do an oil change to a competent mechanic who could completely rebuild an engine.

From Bill I learned far more than just technical knowledge, I also learned about self-confidence, discipline, quality, and craftsmanship.

Developing people requires more than simply recognizing potential, it requires having faith in someone else and taking a risk on them. At first, I made innumerable mistakes and experienced failure on almost a daily basis. Developing me into a real mechanic cost Bill money; especially the time that I accidentally drove his Jeep through a glass garage door. But it was all a price that Bill was willing to pay so that in the future I could add real value to his operation and keep it running when he wasn't around. He knew that there was no guarantee that I would stay. I could have gone to other places, but I felt loyal to the man who had believed in me and I worked hard as a result.

The time is right for rethinking how we go about developing internal talent because people's attitudes towards work are changing – younger generations especially. Employees are hungry for more than a paycheck and tired of office politics. If we are going to spend 1/3 of our life in an office, they say, please let it count for something. They want to contribute in a meaningful way, they want to be developed and experience growth in their professional lives. They want to be invested in and have someone take an interest in them. In return they will be engaged employees seeking ways to add value, rather than to extract it.

It's up to us, as leaders, to spot those who are far from reaching their potential and encouraging them to take the first step towards their own development. We need to stop complaining about not being able to find the right people and spend money investing in the employees we have. We need to stop rewarding people who are good at manipulating others and are climbing a corporate ladder solely for the purpose of boosting their own ego. We need to be hands-on teachers and get intentional about helping people grow. Only by taking risks on individuals and making a sustained effort will we be able to unlock the full potential of human capital that lies dormant in our organizations.

Sterling Leadership Trait #8: Has and Shares a Compelling Vision

37 Signals is a very unusual company. It started out as a web design company and transformed itself into a software company, almost by accident, when the project management software product it developed for internal use (called Basecamp) became extremely

popular outside of the company. Without a single salesperson, 37signals had soon signed up thousands of customers. Unlike most software companies, 37signals is based in Chicago versus Silicon Valley and frequently turns down extravagant offers from venture capital firms and private equity groups to buy them out because that's not the vision that those within the company have or had when they started it.

The uniqueness and unusualness of the company is a direct result of its very unique and unusual leader, Jason Fried. Fried is well known for his unconventional thinking and the seriousness with which he takes leadership, values, and culture. Fried lets most of his 45 employees work remotely from cities across the world. He recommends throwing customer requests for new features in the trashcan (the best suggestions will keep cropping up again and again.) He thinks that making financial projections is a waste of time. He says that meetings are toxic. He fires workaholics. While Fried is a contrarian, he's not when it comes to vision and its absolute necessity for guiding a company to greatness.

But in February, Fried made an announcement that surprised even those familiar with him and his company:

*"Moving forward, we will be a one product
company. That product will be Basecamp. Our
entire company will rally around Basecamp.
Basecamp is our best idea and our biggest
winner. We've had other big hits, but nothing
quite like Basecamp."*

He went on to explain why they made this decision:

*"We've released so many products over the years,
we've become a bit scattered, a bit diluted.
Nobody does their best work when they're spread
too thin. We do our best work when we're all
focused on one thing. Further, we've always
enjoyed being a small company. So while we
could hire a bunch more people to do a bunch
more things, that kind of rapid expansion is at
odds with our culture. We want to maintain the
kind of company where everyone knows
everyone's name. That's one of the reasons why
so many of the people who work at 37signals
stay at 37signals. Last August we conducted a
thorough review of our products, our customer
base, our passions, and <u>our visions of the
company for the next 20 years</u>. When we put it
all on the table, everything lined up and pointed
at one clear conclusion. "*

Jason Fried is still interested in growing his
company, but he's more interested in staying true to
his vision of the type of company they will be and

their collective visions of where they want to go. Fried knows what many leaders don't, which is just how difficult "good growth" is. From a quality and cash flow perspective, rapid growth is tough. Rapid, thoughtless growth can destroy your company in more subtle ways too. The siren song of huge potential and rapid growth has a way of causing leaders to lose sight of their vision and lead their organizations far from the original path they set out on. Once the vision and path are lost, people begin to burn themselves out running in circles and soon they are turning on each other.

Contrary to what most people think, growth is not necessarily good. Before you blindly pursue an opportunity for growth, I would recommend that you ask yourself the following questions:

1. Does this opportunity bring us closer to our vision of where we want to go?
2. Does this opportunity bring us closer to our vision of who we want to be?

If you had unlimited resources, you could pursue every opportunity for growth. But you don't and you can't. Choosing one path will preclude you from taking another. So, let your vision dictate which direction you take.

Humans are constantly telling each other stories – around campfires, in lines at the grocery store, through novels read on airplanes and movies viewed in theatres.

Stories help us to see order in a chaotic world and find meaning in our lives. Stories connect us to the past so that we can understand how we fit into a larger experience and community. Stories help us imagine what the future could be like.

The way that humans are inherently inspired and united by stories makes story telling a very powerful tool. In fact, telling stories is one of the primary ways that cultures are created and influenced. This holds true for corporate culture as well.

Here's an example of a really uninspiring corporate story:

A long time ago the founder of our company started building computers and selling them. Over time the company grew and today we sell lots of computers and phones. As an employee at our company, you can help us to sell even more computers and phones.

Here's an example of the same company's story, but telling it in a more compelling way:

The founder of our company dropped out of college in the 80's to follow his radical dream of making a computer for the average person that was intuitive and fun to use. He and a small group of people literally started the business in a garage. The odds were stacked against them. They lacked money and business experience but still had the courage to compete against enormous companies and challenge paradigms held by almost everyone in the technology industry. It was not easy, and the fledgling company had to overcome innumerable obstacles, but today it is one of the largest and most well-known companies in world. The company relentlessly pushes the envelope of innovation and challenges the status quo because it knows that its many highly capable competitors are desperate to steal any market share that they can. As an employee of our company, you will have the opportunity to help change the world.

The second story is far superior because like all good stories it has an intriguing plot and good characters. People in the organization can see how the company that they are working in is now in a much different place than when it began and how that transformation occurred. They can see how they fit into the story and can contribute to and help write the rest of the story. It is also important to note that the second story helps to *demonstrate* what the values and culture of the company is (innovation, risk-taking, perseverance, etc...)

Who would have thought that being a good leader required being a good storyteller?

Perhaps things are not going well for your organization and you can't fathom how you can transform your organization's dismal situation into a story people would care about or be moved by. Being the leader of a company that is lagging in an industry is tough. The underdog company has to chase scraps of market share, is often on the verge of collapse, and can't afford to hire the most credentialed and experienced individuals. However, by choosing to view the situation from a different perspective we can see it has all the makings of a good story.

Remember the movie *Rocky*? People love rooting for the underdog. It's a story that everyone understands, resonates with, and wants to be a part of. Instead of ignoring or denying your company's situation in the marketplace, embrace it and help your employees and leadership team to find their place in the narrative of the underdog.

If you're really an underdog, none of your competition cares about you. They've left you for dead. That's a good thing. Revel in your obscurity. Devise strategies and bide your time. Let your competitors become complacent and lose touch with their customers, while you prepare for your great comeback. It's said that money easily gained is easily lost. The opposite is also true. When every dollar counts, you spend it as wisely as possible. While your competitors are making frivolous and poorly thought out spending decisions, your organization is becoming lean and fit. In addition to highly disciplined cost controls, an underdog company is also forced to become more creative and resourceful than those in more cash comfortable positions. Instead of throwing money at problems, your team has to actually use its wits, which tends to produce real solutions, not temporary fixes. If the odds are against you, that will make your imminent success even more rewarding.

Whatever your situation, there is always a story to tell.

Sterling Leadership Trait #10: Acknowledges the Unknown but Keeps Moving

Uncertainty is always present in war. No matter the amount of reconnaissance and spying, the commanders of armies never have all the information about each other's troop positions, capabilities and intentions, or even the environments and weather conditions in which they and their troops will have to fight. This frustratingly limited scope of combat reality has frequently been referred to as the Fog of War. Good military leaders are as aware of what they don't know as what they do know because when they overestimate their level of certainty about a particular variable, lives are lost.

Philosophers, our thought leaders, are also keenly aware of the limits of what can be known – they refer to the study of knowing and uncertainty as epistemology. Like good military commanders, our best philosophers make as few assumptions as possible, and when they do have to make them, they explicitly state that they are making them. If the foundation is faulty, the whole structure is liable to fall down, so a philosopher spends most of her efforts on making sure that the foundation of her theory or belief is solid.

Leaders operating in the realm of business should also have a healthy understanding of and respect for uncertainty. External environments can be very foggy. Regulatory environments and tax structures change frequently. The exact size and true demand of a specific market is unknowable before a product is launched into it. The decisions of your competitors are invisible to you until they make them. Even within your own organization, there is plenty of uncertainty. Employee motives and capabilities are sometimes difficult to determine. Untangling conflicts within teams—and getting to the bottom of who was responsible for what—is no easy task.

As a leader, you need to navigate between two extremes, best militarily exemplified by Napoleon Bonaparte and George B. McClellan:

Disregarding Uncertainty (Napoleon Bonaparte)

A healthy dose of awareness and humbleness goes a long way. If you think that the facts no longer matter, or you've been so successful in the past that you can't lose, your own personal Waterloo is only a matter of time.

Paralyzed by Uncertainty (George B. McClellan)

While Robert E. Lee was moving nimbly and cleverly closer to Union territory, McClellan was pouring over maps and wringing his hands. His indecision ended up costing tens of thousands of Union and Confederate lives. If you cannot operate despite some level of ambiguity, you cannot lead.

Leading a team into the unknown means that a leader sometimes has to make educated guesses, risky decisions and quick judgments, some of which will be wrong. This should not be a surprise because the gap between a tidy business plan and the hard facts of reality is more often than not, massive. This is the Fog of Business. Nevertheless, when goals are set and then not met it is the leader who bears the brunt of the responsibility for casting the wrong vision or messing up the execution. Nobody finds it easy to admit failure, especially leaders.

I think that instead of seeing success and failure as our two binary options, leaders need to shift to an attitude of exploration. Entrepreneurs and venture capitalists in Silicon Valley have known this for a long time. So, they've taken a different approach to leadership and strategy. They begin with the assumption that some or most of a leader's predictions and assumptions will be at least partially wrong. A leader's job then is to find out, as quickly as possible, which predictions and assumptions were wrong and why they were wrong. The next task is to take that newly gathered information and use it to make adjustments to the organization itself or the product or service the organization is providing. It is an iterative process. In Silicon Valley it's called pivoting, not failure.

Here are three tips to help you build an organization that can pivot:

1. Communicate with your organization. Make it clear that you know where the organization is headed, but that there is no perfect map or a predetermined path to get there. You will have to find a trail or make one.
2. Create a culture where it's okay to be wrong and people are encouraged to acknowledge reality, instead of obscuring or hiding from it.
3. Formalize how you will collect data, analyze it, disseminate the findings, and modify your business model/product/service in response to what that data tells you. If you're not systematic about it, pivoting won't work.

Instead of talking predominately about success and failure, your organization should be talking about momentum and direction. Are you getting closer or further away from your goal and at what rate? Your organization should be talking about what it has learned and how the things it has learned have changed how the organization operates. Your organization should be talking about what it is going to stop doing today and what it is going to try tomorrow. Keep pivoting towards the goal until your organization is moving swiftly in the right direction.

Humans are natural problem solvers. In fact, we spend a good portion of each day solving problems and for the most part, we're pretty good at it too. That is, as long as the problems are concrete and easy to define. This is why finding an alternate route to work after discovering the road you're on is closed ahead due to construction is an easier problem to solve than motivating a fatiguing project team. The problems that we face within organizations tend to be of the more difficult and abstract variety. They are ambiguous, intermittent, and very seldom have one root cause.

It would be better if more people slowly made their way to conclusions rather than rushing to them. But, many people are very uncomfortable living in the unknown and so they prefer to have a simple story with a quick conclusion (even when it's wrong), which promptly puts their world back into order. So, as leaders detect problems within their organizations or notice that goals are not being met, it is only natural that they will make a beeline to the nearest apparent conclusion and solution.

Arriving at the correct explanation and conclusion is difficult for a couple of reasons.

Despite living in a phenomenally complex world, we gravitate towards simple explanations because they are easier to hold in our heads and because a simple explanation suggests a simple solution. It is also human nature that we want our new stories to agree with and support our old ones, which is basically how a personal bias functions. If some guy in a green shirt stole candy from you when you were a baby, you might have drawn the inference that people who wear green shirts are untrustworthy. From that moment on, you might then begin to subconsciously accept evidence that supports this conclusion and discard evidence that challenges it. Even if biases are incorrect, they can be incredibly hard to overcome.

Can we find a better way to find explanations and arrive at conclusions? How can we walk to conclusions, instead of rush to them?

The only way to get traction and solve problems like these is through structured and disciplined problem solving. The following is a problem solving framework that can be applied to just about any type of organization to tackle almost any issue.

1. **Prioritize and Pursue**
   If you attempt to solve all of the problems that your organization faces at the same time, you'll accomplish nothing. If you focus your energies only on the most recent

problem instead of the most crippling to
your organization, you'll accomplish
nothing. Good leaders engage the whole
organization to develop a list of issues and
then prioritize them in terms of what is
doing the most damage. Pick the top three
and make the commitment not to tackle
other problems until you've solved one of
these.

2. **Discuss the Problem, Not the Solution**
    Invite people who are being directly
    impacted by the problem to discuss the
    problem, but <u>don't let anyone jump ahead
    and start proposing solutions</u>. Just as an
    army commander orders his troops to do
    reconnaissance before launching an attack,
    you need to map out the problem, view it
    from different perspectives, and define it as
    completely as possible, before proposing
    solutions. This needs to be done as
    objectively as possible. Discussing the
    problem first and waiting to propose
    solutions will enable your team to suspend
    their judgments, biases and assumptions and
    see the problem as it is, not as they want or
    fear it to be.

3. **Searching for Solutions**

I remember my first boss, Bill Paberzs, telling me that there were two types of mechanics in the world: those who just start replacing parts until the problem is fixed and those who actually diagnose a car's malfunction in order to precisely address the problem. As leaders, we want to be like the latter. After your team has thoroughly described and understood the problem, you can begin diagnosing the problem and searching for the most elegant and effective solution.

4. **Get Buy-in**

   Everyone involved needs to come to an agreement on the proposed solution, and if not, explain why they don't agree. Buy-in is important, because without it people are pulling in different directions, which is probably the least productive thing that a team can do.

5. **Assign Tasks and Provide Resources**

   A meeting should always end with *specific* tasks assigned to *specific* people. If no tasks are assigned, all you did was have a nice talk. However, don't forget that people need the correct tools and the necessary resources to complete their work. Make sure they have them.

6. **Monitor progress weekly**
   Hold your team accountable and have your
   team hold you accountable. Missed
   deadlines and lack of follow-through sow
   the seeds of chaos in an organization and set
   a terrible precedent.

Analyzing and solving problems in this manner is
an iterative process that requires patience and
discipline that does not come easily. As a leader, it
is not only your responsibility to practice this type
of constructive problem solving yourself, but to
embed these methodologies in the culture of your
company. The truth is, few things are as rewarding
as solving a tough problem and getting traction. If
you can show your team that this methodology
works, those around you will be eager to apply the
same principles.

*Sterling Leadership Trait #12: Knows the Difference
Between Talking and Communicating*

Communicating, or attempting to communicate, is
something that we've all been doing since as long as
we can remember. For this reason, many of us
assume that we have mastered communication and

seldom think about what exactly we are doing when we are communicating. So, let's just step back a minute and think about what communication is. Communication is the process of bundling up the thoughts in your brain into packages called words and sending them (via speaking, email, etc.) to another person who has to then unbundle those packages (words) and interpret them as best they can. Good communication exists when the thoughts that were formed in your brain have been replicated in someone else's brain with minimal distortion. One would think that if you had a clearly formed idea or concept in your brain and the correct words to describe it, the process of getting that same idea into someone else's brain would be easy. However there is something else that you need to take into account when you're communicating and it is what linguists and communication experts refer to as "noise" or "interference."

In order to understand what this interference is and how it gets in the way of communication, we have to understand the nature of words – those devices that we use to package up ideas. Words are tools and imperfect ones at that. They are tags that we stick onto reality. When I say the word "chair" we all probably know what I mean by that. However, if I say the word "honorable" we may have a far more difficult time agreeing on what that particular word means. The more abstract the thing I'm trying to describe, the more difficulty we will have agreeing on what is meant by that word. The same word can mean many different things to many different people. Now, once you start stringing them together into sentences and paragraphs and combining them with body language, their meaning can become very difficult for the person receiving the message to interpret correctly.

How is it then that the same word or sentence can be interpreted so differently by two different people?

History

Every conversation has a history. Think of someone that you've known for a long time. You've had many, many conversations with this person and because of that you can make certain assumptions and choices when you have conversations with them in the future. You can leave a lot unsaid because you are essentially picking up from where you last left off. Also, people who have known each other for a long time don't need to spend much time figuring out what the other means when they use words and phrases that describe abstract concepts. In a sense, it is like they are sharing a dictionary in which they have both agreed on the meaning of each word, symbol, and phrase. People who have known each other for a long time can also avoid the use of certain words and phrases that the other party may find upsetting or counterproductive to the transmission of the message. When you communicate with someone who you don't know very well, you run the risk of assuming they know what you mean and you also run the risk of saying a word or phrase that has a very negative connotation to them which they may have obtained from a past conversation you weren't aware of.

Context

When you talk to someone, you enter into that person's system of meaning. The person you are communicating with grew up in a particular part of the country, during a particular time in history, was raised by a particular family, belongs to a particular economic class, and has a particular education. All of these different factors create in that person a very particular system of meaning. If you and the person you are communicating with are very similar, then chances are you will be able to communicate very effectively. They will probably interpret your words, phrases, and sentences with minimal contextual interference.

Non-verbal Cues

Another complexity to add to the concept of communication is the fact that we don't use only words to communicate. There's body language. Crossing of the arms, direct eye contact, leaning back, and fidgeting all communicate a message. Messages can also be insinuated by saying certain things in the presence of certain people or by choosing to respond quickly or slowly to an email. Our non-verbal communication can reinforce the message we are trying to get across or obstruct it.

So, how do good communicators communicate?

First of all, good communicators make a conscious decision to share the ideas that are residing in their brains with all the other brains in their organization. This means ensuring not only that their direct reports get it, but also that key messages are communicated faithfully throughout the organization. When people are left in the dark, no matter where they are in the organization, they tend to feel excluded and unengaged. Secondly, good communicators attempt to empathize with those who are different from them. Most leaders are communicating with a broad array of people from different backgrounds, cultures, and generations. By being cognizant of the different histories and contexts of those within their organization, good communicators are able to step outside their own narrow perspective and imagine how their words and sentences might be misinterpreted by or resonate with different groups of people. They modify the delivery of their message accordingly. Lastly, good communicators realize that good communication is best understood and practiced as two or more parties working to arrive at a shared meaning, not as a simple linear process between a sender and receiver. Good communicators are always asking and listening for feedback so that they can clarify their message.

Effective communication is one of the primary skills that every leader must have. Casting a vision, getting buy-in, creative problem solving, motivating, teaching, delegating - good communication is at the heart of each of these activities. It does not matter how extensive your vocabulary is or how confident of a speaker you are, if you cannot communicate effectively, you cannot lead effectively.

Sterling Leadership Trait #13: Can Empathize

One of the greatest and most challenging characteristics of humanity is that we are all different:

What is easy for one person may be difficult for another.

What one person loves another can't stand.

What motivates one person may be the very thing that discourages someone else.

What one person values another couldn't care less about.

For example, imagine a CEO walks into a staff meeting and announces to her team that the company has exceeded its quarterly financial goals, so together they need to decide how to use the excess profits. The CEO asks for a show of hands to determine whether the profits should be distributed as cash bonuses or used to purchase new furniture for the whole office. It's a split vote and the CEO is astonished to see her team of usually subdued professionals begin arguing and shouting over one another.

Finally, someone louder than everyone else shouts in frustration, "Who gives a *$#&!* about furniture?"

The core of this argument isn't really about furniture though; it's about differences in what people value. Take a look at the following list and take a guess at which of the following values are probably a big deal to the people who voted for the new furniture. What values might be important to those who voted for a raise?

Fairness	Balance	Autonomy	Self-reliance	Loyalty	Security	Order
Creativity	Merit	Openness	Optimism	Perfection	Teamwork	Solitude
Status	Strength	Success	Results	Sacrifice	Reciprocity	Adventure
Compassion	Diversity	Equality	Excellence	Atmosphere	Skill	Sincerity
Beauty	Gratitude	Relaxation	Honesty	Peace	Exploration	Discipline

One of the worst things you can say to someone is, "That's a stupid value." Values are rarely stupid because most of the time they're very well informed by an individual's beliefs and past experiences. When you say that someone's values are stupid, you're being insensitive about both of these aspects of a person, as the triangle below helps to illustrate:

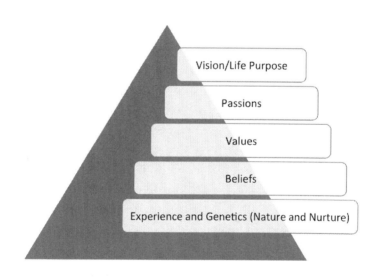

On of the biggest determinants of someone's values is the generation they belong to. A population that shared a common historical experience will tend to be affected by that shared experience in a similar way. This may cause them to see the world through the same lens. While this concept has been at times abused or overextended, everyone has witnessed first-hand the conflicts and misunderstandings that seem to result from generational differences. This is an important concept for you to understand because there's a good chance that you lead an organization in which individuals who identify themselves as Baby Boomers, Generation X, and Generation Y, see the world in radically different ways.

Just so we're all on the same page, let's review the most common generational groups in an organization today:

Baby Boomers – 1946-1964

*In general, baby boomers are associated with a rejection or **redefinition of traditional values**; however, many commentators have disputed the extent of that rejection, noting the widespread continuity of values with older and younger generations. In Europe and North America boomers are widely associated with **privilege**, as many grew up in a time of **affluence**. One of the features of Boomers was that they tended to*

think of themselves as a special generation,
very different from those that had come before
them.

Generation X – 1965-1980

The 2011 publication "The Generation X
*Report", finds that Gen Xers are **highly***
***educated, active, balanced, happy** and family*
***oriented.** The study dispels the materialistic,*
slacker, disenfranchised stereotype associated
with youth in the 1970 and 80s. In the preface
to Generation X Goes Global: Mapping a Youth
Culture in Motion, a collection of global essays,
Professor Christine Henseler summarizes it as "a
*generation whose **worldview is based on***
***change**, on the need to combat corruption,*
*dictatorships, abuse, **AIDS, a generation in***
search of human dignity and individual
***freedom**, the need for stability, love, tolerance,*
and human rights for all."

Millennials 1980 – 2000

Jean Twenge, the author of the 2006
book Generation Me, *considers Millennials*
along with younger Gen Xers to be part of what
she calls "Generation Me". Twenge attributes
***confidence** and **tolerance** to the Millennials but*
*also a sense of entitlement and **narcissism** based*
on personality surveys that showed
increasing narcissism among Millennials

compared to preceding generations when they
were teens and in their twenties. Studies
predict that Millennials will switch jobs
frequently, holding many more jobs
than <u>Generation X</u> *due to their **great***
expectations.

The point here is not that someone can be entirely understood based on how old they are, in what kind of household they grew up in, or where they are from. The point is that we can reduce conflict, build trust, and better motivate people if we suspend our judgments about their values and try to see the world from their perspective and make decisions accordingly. This is empathy and as the workforce becomes more diverse, it will only become more critical.

Sterling Leadership Trait #14: Knows What Really Drives Us

If you could craft the perfect incentive structure for your employees, would you still need to lead and manage them? There are those who would have us believe that it is possible to put in place a system of monetary incentives and disincentives to motivate and perfectly guide the decision making of a team –

thus making leadership and management unnecessary. Making an organization successful is just a matter of implementing the right carrots and sticks, say the proponents of this concept. It does seem logical. However, in this case, our intuitions about how to motivate people are completely wrong. I became convinced of this after I read *Drive* by Daniel Pink. Pink makes an extremely compelling case for why it is time to put down our carrots and sticks and leave them behind in the 20th century were they belong. How he arrived at that conclusion is fascinating as well, because it had nothing to do with touchy-feely ideas or a socialist agenda but instead cold, hard empirical facts.

The Federal Reserve Bank, the University of Chicago, and the London School of Economics are all institutions that believe in checking the basic assumptions on which their ideologies rest. So, in recent years they've all conducted extensive social experiments to determine if incentives work the way most people intuitively believe them to work. Which is to say, using a monetary reward system to encourage the behavior you want more of and punish the behavior you want less of. One such social experiment was relatively simple but yielded results that stunned the researchers conducting it. Basically, they gave a group of MIT students various tasks to complete and then provided three levels of monetary rewards to incentivize them –

management 101, right? What they discovered was that as long as the task required mechanical skill, the system worked. The greater the monetary reward, the better the performance. But, once the task called for even rudimentary cognitive and creative skill, *the larger reward led to poorer performance.* The researchers thought that perhaps they needed to rerun the experiment in a place where the monetary rewards would be considered more significant, so they went to India. In that experiment, the highest level of incentive was equivalent to two times an individuals' monthly income. The results were the same. The higher the monetary incentives, the worse the performance.

What can explain this result that seems to run counter to any logical explanation?

Pink posits, and I agree with him, that financial incentives tend to dull thinking, hamper creativity, and restrict our minds. We are focusing on the money, not the problem. So, the first part of the solution is to do what Pink calls, "taking the money off the table" by making sure that people have enough of it. When employees are paid generously they can stop obsessing about their lack of money and focus on the task at hand.

The next step is to appeal to individuals' intrinsic motivations. There are three of them: autonomy, mastery, and purpose.

Autonomy

People have ideas and passions they want to pursue. As much as possible, let them. Each person also has a specific way they want to accomplish their work and go about solving problems, so as much as possible, let them. To illustrate this point, Pink talks about Google's policy that allows employees to use 20% of their time to work on and develop their own ideas. Half of Google's new product ideas have come from this 20% time. Technology companies are becoming extremely flexible in other ways. Increasingly, employees are being allowed to create their own schedules and form their own teams. They are being evaluated on what they produce, not how much time they are at their desks. They are being respected for how well they can solve problems, not follow instructions.

Mastery

Whether it is playing golf or an instrument, people love to get better at doing challenging things. In a corporate environment, individuals find motivation in mastery too, whether that be building complex financial models or conducting large-scale marketing research. The long process of becoming really good at something is itself a reward and makes us feel good about ourselves.

Purpose

People want their work to count for something. They are eager to work and contribute in the service of something other and larger than themselves. The best talent is flocking to places like Google and Tesla Motors not primarily for the compensation, but for what those places represent and the meaning in their own lives that those organizations can give them.

The best way to motivate people on an assembly line is still with monetary incentives. But with regards to motivating knowledge workers, our intuitions have failed us. In this day and age, humans need to be engaged, not manipulated. We need to foster creative and dynamic thinking, not stifle it. So pay your team well, and create an environment were autonomy, mastery, and purpose is possible.

Sterling Leadership Trait #15: Builds an Organization, Not a Cult

When was the last time that one person out of your entire management team expressed a view in disagreement with everyone else, and stood by their conviction?

The fact is it's usually easier for people to go with the flow rather than rock the boat and it's more common to think that things will stay the same than change. This is how Groupthink takes root. Groupthink is a psychological phenomenon that occurs within a group of people, in which the desire for harmony or conformity in the group results in an incorrect or deviant decision-making outcome.

After the Yom Kippur War in 1973, in which Israel was nearly overrun by a coordinated surprise attack by Egypt and Syria, the Israeli Military Intelligence Directorate began investigating weaknesses within their own organizations. Why had they thought the possibility for invasion so remote? Why had warning signs and suspicious activity near their borders previous to the attack not elicited more concern from the defense department? Why had those who had concerns not vocalized them? How had leadership become so complacent? One of their key findings was that groupthink had infected the leadership of the military and intelligence departments.

So, in order to combat this weakness, a special task force was formed to begin cultivating a new culture of openness and diversity of ideas, guided by the slogan "Freedom of opinion, discipline in action." But, they did far more to overhaul their organization's culture than come up with a catchy phrase. On the institutional-level they established a "devil's advocate" office whose sole job it was to criticize conventional thinking and the analysis of other departments. This special office was well funded and supplied with highly experienced individuals from diverse backgrounds who were given the authority to ask tough questions. On the individual level, analysts were given channels for expressing alternate opinions, in which they are free to critique the conclusions of their superiors and departments. Their superiors were in turn encouraged not to criticize analysts who wrote such memos.

This strategy worked for a nation, but how well could it be applied to a business? How can a company remain open and permit healthy criticism without destroying confidence in the leadership (or, in other words, maintain "freedom of opinion and discipline in action)?

I would suggest the following three guidelines:

1. The leadership team needs to remain united in their collective pursuit of the company's vision, mission, and core values. This is (almost) non-negotiable and guarded like

the keep of the castle. These things can change, but it should be about as difficult as amending the Constitution.

2. Create proper channels for open communication throughout the organization and ensure that people dare to use them. These are like pressure valves; if you don't have them you're going to be faced with an explosion. Or, if not that, passive aggressive employees will be sowing seeds of dissent and undermining your efforts.

3. According to Irving Janis (an anti-groupthink guru): Consider starting discussions with your leadership team by asking the least senior director or manager to give their opinion first. Or, have larger groups split into smaller groups to discuss issues separately before discussing all together.

Building an impactful business does not require a leader of unquestioned authority surrounded by eager yes-men, but it does require a corporate culture that embraces new ideas, change, and keen insights and these things can only exist in an open environment where unconventional thinking can be allowed to exist.

Sterling Leadership Trait #16: Recognizes
Organizational Poison

In the Western world we celebrate and value individuality. The impact that a single person can have on history, culture, or an organization has been demonstrated by the likes of Martin Luther King Jr., Pablo Picasso, and Steve Jobs. These individuals catalyzed positive change and introduced others to new ways of thinking. The reality though is that it is much easier, and more common for an individual to tear down than to build up. The old adage, "Any mule can kick down a barn. It takes a carpenter to build one", rings true more than ever in our present age where negativity and cynicism are so prevalent. The book *Remarkable!*, mentions two types of employees who are potentially the most destructive to an organization: naysayers and self-victimizers. When negativity and self-victimization become an overriding and permanent aspect of someone's character, that individual can inflict an immense amount of damage on an organization.

Naysayers: A naysayer always has or is looking for a reason why something won't work or is not possible. They consistently deny, refuse, or oppose new initiatives and ideas. Naysayers create a negative aura that saps the energy of everyone around them.

Self-victimizers: This is a person who constantly fabricates victimhood for a variety of reasons such as to shift responsibility to others or as a coping strategy. Because self-victimizers take no responsibility for their actions or current situation, they are incapable of looking for solutions that require themselves to change or take initiative. For the self-victimizer, the solution is always up to someone else.

Naysayers and self-victimizers short-circuit the leadership teams' attempts to create an effective organizational culture. According to *Remarkable!*, empowering employees by entrusting them with the responsibility to solve problems and maximizing each individual's autonomy are the key ingredients necessary for an engaged workforce. Coercion has no place in such a culture. Leaders can do their best to create an environment that is conducive for employee engagement and contribution, but, ultimately it is up to each individual to take control of their own destiny and the destiny of the organization that they work within. Thus, individuals have the power and freedom to do something or nothing. Each individual must genuinely believe that they really can make a difference, attempt it and then take responsibility for the outcome. Naysayers and self-victimizers can't do this. They *believe* that they are powerless to positively impact their world and so they *are* powerless to positively impact their world.

Leaders need to take the threat that naysayers and self-victimizers pose to an organization with the utmost seriousness because both mentalities are incredibly contagious and addictive. Like a vicious disease, the mentality of naysayers and self-victimizers can infect and spread throughout an organization's culture with incredible speed, rendering the entire organization paralyzed by defeatism and lost in dense fog of negativity. The cure for such a cultural ailment is far more expensive than the cost of its prevention. For this reason, every effort must be made to quickly convince naysayers and self-victimizers to embrace a more positive worldview or, for the good of the organization, they must be removed from the organization.

Sterling Leadership Trait #17: Understands Sustainability

The necessity and nobleness of working far more than 40 hours per week is something that many people believe with almost religious fervor. It is not uncommon to hear employees brag about the number of consecutive 80-hour weeks they have worked and their lack of sleep as a result. Leaving the office at 5:00 is considered almost a cardinal sin and going home early is practically unforgivable. Owners, directors, and managers have an even more fanatical attachment to working late nights and weekends. It is believed that their responsibilities and paychecks necessitate and justify such behavior. Their holy relics are empty boxes of take-out stacked on conference room tables, discarded coffee cups littering their desks, and the toothbrushes they carry to work. This, however, is a false religion. Recent studies, economic history, and a little bit of common sense reveal that consistently working more than 40 hours per week kills productivity, reduces profitability, and can even risk the survival of an organization.

According to Sara Robinson writing for Salon, it didn't take long for some of the first industrialists to learn this lesson. Pressure from unions in the early 1800's introduced the idea that there was a need to put limits on the amount of work that employees could perform per week. By the mid-1800's the British Parliament had enacted a law which capped the hours per day that an employee could work at 10 hours. The result was that the total output per-worker per day increased. Think about that. People were working less and producing more. Business leaders took note. In the early 1900's, Henry Ford began running his own controlled experiments at his factories to see how the amount of hours an employee worked impacted their productivity. The results where convincing enough that in 1914, Ford doubled his workers' pay and cut their shifts from 9 hours a day to 8. Although initially skeptical of such "radical" decisions, Ford's competitors soon saw that it was a smart business decision and followed suit.

Robinson goes on to state that:

In 1937, the 40-hour week was enshrined nationwide as part of the New Deal. By that point, there were a solid five decades of industrial research that proved, beyond a doubt, that if you wanted to keep your workers bright, healthy, productive, safe and efficient over a sustained stretch of time, you kept them to no more than 40 hours a week and eight hours a day.

Somewhere between then and now, this lesson in productivity was largely forgotten. De-unionization and the false belief that people who are passionate about their work should stay at their desks day and night has reestablished the myth of

The Virtue of Working More Hours. There are a few companies today that are resisting this pervasive fiction. One such example that I read about recently is Openview Venture Partners. Scott Maxwell, the company's founder, got his start working for McKinsey in the early 90's and it was there that his boss challenged the corporate culture of long hours and weekend work. He explained to Maxwell that for religious reasons he only ever worked 6 days instead of 7, unlike all the other employees, and yet he always got more done than them. Maxwell took the lesson to heart and when he started Openview Venture Partners he created and enforced the rule that people couldn't work late, or on the weekends, and he was adamant that when employees went on vacation they weren't allowed to check their emails or call the office. The result? More work got done, the quality of work was higher, and everyone was happier.

How is it possible that working too many hours actually hurts companies more than it helps?

Mistakes – The more tired we get the more mistakes we make. More mistakes means more time spent doing rework. The more rework we spend our time doing, the less efficiently we are using our time and this reduces profitability.

Errors in Judgment – Investigators looking into the Exxon Valdez oil spill and the Challenger explosion discovered that both of these tragedies were, in large part, due to the poor decision making of overworked employees. While errors in your judgment and the judgment of your team might not result in lost lives or millions of barrels of oil spilling into the sea, they can be extremely costly.

Parkinson's Law – Parkinson's Law is the adage that work expands so as to fill the time available for its completion. If the expectation at a place of employment is that everyone is going to work 12 hours a day, then people will in no way be incentivized to find efficient ways to complete their work. This generates a very harmful corporate culture in which time spent in a chair is valued more than new ideas for how to work better. This is a shame, because finding ways to work smarter and not harder is one of the best ways that companies can increase their profits.

Burnout – Working too much for too long will burn anyone out, no matter their age, personality, or health. Burned out individuals leave or are let go when it becomes apparent that they aren't performing well. New employees must be found, interviewed, acclimated, and trained. When they are burned out the cycle repeats. This churn and burn cycle is costly and, not to mention, just plain wrong.

Personal Problems that Become Work Problems – Spending too much time at the office has a negative impact on other parts of our lives as well. Friends, spouses, and family members feel neglected when we work too much and this sows the seeds of conflict. When these relationships become tumultuous it then affects our work, which in turn puts more stress on our fraying relationships.

Consistently working long hours should be seen as a sign of leadership's failure, not a badge of honor. Humans need a balanced rhythm. Work, rest. Work, rest. Work, rest. It's how we are wired, and living in accordance with this truth is important for leaders and those whom they lead. Ignore this rhythm of work and rest and you and your whole organization are liable to seize up like an over-revved engine.

Sterling Leadership Trait #18: Understands What Tears Teams Apart

The recently released spy film, *A Most Wanted Man* centers on a small German intelligence group headed up by Gunther Bachmann (played by Phillip Seymour Hoffman) who is tasked with tracking and disrupting Islamic terrorist groups operating in

Germany. Set in the gloomy city of Hamburg, the film's opening explains that it was here that the 9/11 attacks were planned for years with virtually no interference from German or American intelligence agencies. Although there were many reasons for suspicion and investigation prior to the terrorist attacks, both the German and American organizations did not respond effectively to them because of a lack of coordination and rivalries between and across governmental agencies.

At one point in the movie, Bachmann and his American counterpart discuss why they both work in this stressful and oftentimes brutal espionage environment. Bachmann states that he is committed to the goal of "making the world a safer place", and the American says the same. Yet, despite this shared vision, Bachmann becomes increasingly at odds with not only the American intelligence team, but also his colleagues working in different departments at the German agency. It is clear that despite the common threat hanging over both countries, some of the worst aspects of human nature are powerfully at work hindering a unified response and a team mentality.

Large organizations, such as intelligence agencies, must be organized into departments. Why is it so hard for those various departments to work together effectively? The film provides some interesting insights into why this is:

Us versus Them Mentality

Bachmann leads a group of five people. From their interactions with each other, it is obvious that they have been working together for a long time and are extremely close. They trust Bachmann completely and they have great faith in one another because they have a deep knowledge of each other's abilities and motives. Bachmann's team keeps itself socially and professionally closed off from the other intelligence groups, and even physically isolated in their own facility – only rarely do they cross paths with their colleagues in different departments. By becoming so insular, Bachmann's team makes it nearly impossible for other intelligence groups to trust and work with them and vice versa.

Failure to Build Broad Consensus

Bachmann is a brilliant analyst and spy handler, but he's a terrible salesman. When superiors call him to a meeting to explain why he's waiting to take a terrorist suspect in, he's standoffish, cold and evasive. Present at the meeting are a number of folks that it is clear Bachmann doesn't like, and he lets them know it. He struggles to communicate his methods and motives in a direct way and opts instead for making an analogy about fishing for sharks, which no one but himself seems to find amusing. Instead of winning his superiors and colleagues over to his side during this crucial moment, he mostly just angers and annoys them.

Old Wounds

Numerous characters throughout the film make allusions to some operation that Bachmann botched in Beirut years ago, which led to the deaths of several operatives. Ostensibly, this past failure was the result of Bachmann trusting someone too much who later betrayed him. Haunted by this fact and the inability of any of his colleagues to let him forget it and move on, Bachmann is paranoid to the point of trusting no one outside of his innermost circle. His past cripples his ability to coordinate with other departments.

Putting Personal Gain over the Interests of the Organization

As Bachmann and his team work their way up the terrorist network, it becomes ever more tempting for other departments and team members to capture these terrorists instead of turning them into informants, who can then supply information necessary to capture higher value targets. Although all the German and American intelligence agents claim that their only goal is to "make the world a safer place" that conviction is put to the test when those same agents realize that being able to take credit for capturing a low level terrorist is better for their individual careers than using the "asset" to help another department capture an even higher value terrorist.

The world of espionage is very different from the one most of us work in every day, but many of the same factors preventing optimal coordination and teamwork exist in every organization, regardless of the field or industry. Resisting cliquishness, learning to build a broad consensus, freeing people from their past mistakes, and properly incentivizing the attainment of group goals are all ways to break down the divisions that keep our organizations from working together.

Sterling Leadership Trait #19: Embraces Change

The seasoned inventor and futurist Ray Kurzweil says a lot of things that sound crazy, and then end up coming true – with remarkable accuracy. He foresaw many key technological breakthroughs well before they occurred, such as the ubiquity of the internet, a computer beating a world champion at chess, face-recognition software, and self-driving cars. Currently, he's working as Google's Director of Engineering, tasked with getting computers to understand human language. His predictions for the next 20 years include radical visions such as artificial intelligence that is smarter than humans and nanobots traveling within our bloodstreams identifying and destroying cancer cells.

The reason that Kurzweil can make such bold statements about the (relatively) near future is that he believes the rate of technological change is accelerating. Up until recently, technology advanced in a linear fashion, but he posits that from here on out it will continue to be exponential. Moore's Law, which basically states that computing power doubles every two years, has been extremely consistent (predictable) and is the underlying driver for why Kurzweil believes that technological evolution and advancement can happen in shorter and shorter intervals.

If you're still not convinced that we are in for some major changes in the next 5 to 10 years, consider the following examples of how the future is already arriving:

- Fusion: For nearly 50 years, physicists have been trying to use energy to fuse atoms together (fusion), instead of splitting them apart (fission). A fusion reactor would generate virtually unlimited amounts of energy very cheaply and with no negative impact on the environment. Lockheed Martin's Skunk Works Department claims that they're working on a fusion reactor and that it is 5 years out from being a commercially viable product.[6]

- 3D Printers: The 3D printing industry is developing rapidly. Not only is it now possible to print complex metal and plastic objects on demand with amazing precision, but we can expect to see the first printed human organ this year.[7]

- Artificial Intelligence: Deep Blue, IBM's chess playing super computer, beat the chess Grandmaster Gary Kasparov in 1997. 14 years later, IBM built Watson, which soundly defeated two long-standing *Jeopardy!* champions at their own game on live television.[8]

- Genomic Sequencing: If scientists can understand which genetic mutations cause diseases, they can, in theory, correct those genes and eliminate the disease. Since the first human genome was sequenced in 2003, the cost of doing this process has dropped precipitously – from one billion dollars 10 years ago, to one thousand dollars today.[9]

- Advanced materials – Graphene is the thinnest, strongest, lightest, and most conductive material on earth. The first crystals of graphene were discovered in 2004 by two scientists in Manchester, for which they received the Nobel Prize in physics in 2010. Graphene's unique set of properties have applications for nearly every industry.[10]

It is up to you to judge whether technological advancements, like those listed above, represent opportunities or threats. We can't stop the world from changing, but we can change our own perspective, so that instead of being paralyzed by the fear of change we can seek out opportunities. Only leaders with the right perspective and sufficient imagination and vision will be able to get ahead of this rapidly changing curve.

Kodak's story exemplifies both the way that a company can embrace change and also resist it. By diligently investing in cutting-edge technology and introducing innovative products, Kodak was able to capture nearly 90% of the American photographic film market by the mid 70's. Its logo was as recognizable as McDonald's' and the phrase "Kodak moment" worked its way into the American lexicon. Around that same time, at the pinnacle of its market dominance, a Kodak scientist developed the first digital camera. Kodak executives took a look at the bulky device, called it "cute", and handed it back to its inventor. They had no idea that they had just been handed the future of photography and the disrupting technology that would ultimately destroy their company. The sad thing is that Kodak's collapse didn't happen fast – at least, not at first. It took three decades, with many missed opportunities to adapt its business model to the new technology that was changing its environment forever.

All living organisms use their nervous systems to sense changes and threats in their environment and respond. If the changes or threats cannot be responded to effectively, species then either adapt or die. Similar to organisms, organizations that survive sense what's going on in their environments and respond or adapt. Really effective organizations do something even better though. They anticipate how their environment will change and plan accordingly. Kodak actually did a reasonable job of sensing its environment. In 1981, when Sony introduced the first digital camera to the market, the Kodak's leadership assembled a marketing team to assess the threat. The marketing team made a presentation in which they stated that Kodak had about 10 years before digital cameras would do serious damage to Kodak's core business. But, it was as if Kodak were a deer frozen in the headlights of a car that was still 100 miles away. Change proved too difficult for Kodak's leadership to execute. The individuals were smart, the organization was stupid and Kodak died.

Our economic, social, and political environment is about to be transformed by computers that can understand spoken language, cars that drive themselves, 3D printers that can make parts out of plastic and metal on demand, robots that can be taught how to perform rote tasks, software that writes news stories, modified algae that excretes petroleum, gene therapies that repair faulty DNA, etc... Fortunes will be won and lost faster than ever before. Kodak had 30 years to change and failed to do so. Our organizations will have far less time.

Sterling Leadership Trait #20: Can Sell

Arthur Miller's play, Death of a Salesman, is one of the reasons I never considered a career in sales. The image of the burned out main character, Willy Loman, wearily stumbling through a door, carrying an enormous suitcase in each hand, was enough to convince me that sales was all to often brutal and thankless work. But Dan Pink, in his book *To Sell Is*

Human, makes a compelling case that *we are all already in sales*. He explains, "When I sat down to deconstruct my own workdays, I discovered that I spend a sizable portion of them selling in a broader sense – persuading, influencing, and convincing others." This is what's known as non-sales selling. According to a Gallup poll that Pink sites, people are now spending about 40% of their time at work engaged in non-sales selling. If you're a leader, you are probably spending even more than 40% of your time doing this type of work – trying to influence internal and external groups of people, encouraging those around you to embrace change, convincing a job candidate to join your organization, and persuading individuals to work together toward a common cause.

At its core, selling is the act of convincing or persuading others to give up something they value for something you have. Defining sales this way explains why despite the fact that we are all already in sales (leaders especially) selling isn't easy. To learn how to sell better, Pink interviewed social scientists, read stacks of behavioral economic research papers, and tagged along with top salespeople in order to learn their secrets. From the knowledge he gleaned from these sources he determined that all good sales people are attuned and buoyant.

Attunement means "bringing oneself into alignment with individuals, groups, and contexts." This requires seeing situations through the eyes of others and adapting what we say and do to be sensitive to those whom we are trying to persuade or convince. Not only does this lower the probability of offending individuals and groups but it also enables you to find a unique and powerful way to best connect with your audience.

Buoyancy means that we expect opposition and engage with it in a positive way. Salespeople face rejection and disappointment every day, but by employing psychological strategies, they are able to persevere until they are successful. Pink mentions several of these strategies in the book, but the one I find most compelling is simply remembering that if you truly believe in what you are selling, you'll always have the strength to keep pushing forward.

The last section of Pink's book describes specific things you can do to boost your sales success rate. He argues that with people's attentions spans constantly shrinking, it is increasingly important to distill the essence of your message down to the length of a Tweet, or even a single word. Pink also recommends making pitches personal and purposeful, which means that coldly worded corporate edicts handed down from on high are about the worst way to sell an idea or policy change. Communicating openly and in person with those in your organization, and explaining how your ideas fit meaningfully into the bigger picture are both key characteristics of a pitch that will make it stick.

It is tempting to think that persuasion and convincing are unnecessary for the top leaders in an organization because of the power inherent in their positions. But this is untrue because it ignores the importance of buy in. The difference between the employees who are *just following* orders and those who *actually believe* in the orders is immense. This is why, if you're in leadership, you also need to be in sales.

Sterling Leadership Trait #21: Shapes the Organization's Culture

Japan's post-WWII economic growth through the 1980's appeared to be nothing short of miraculous to the outside observer. Could it be that the nation's culture had been primarily responsible for transforming a small, resource poor island country into the second largest economy in the world? And do companies, like nations, have distinct cultures too? According to Gareth Morgan, in his book *Images of Organization*, it was the difficulty that the West had competing with Japan during the eighties that sparked a sudden interest among managers and academics to better understand organizational culture and how it might be re-shaped and designed in order to produce spectacular results.

I believe that corporate culture is a critical concept that my clients must understand, especially in the complex globalized world we live in today. Throughout my career as an engineer and executive coach in West Michigan, I have seen first-hand how a corporate culture can either unlock human potential or constrain it.

One of the reasons many leaders understand company culture so poorly is that the concept is quite abstract. So let's try to gain a clearer understanding of what exactly it is we're talking about.

Ravasi and Schultz (2006) state that organizational culture is a set of shared mental assumptions that guide interpretation and action in organizations by defining appropriate behavior for various situations. Put even more succinctly by McKinsey & Company, company culture is: "how we do things around here."

Here's a more concrete illustration: Joe was responsible for developing and rolling out a new product. Despite his best efforts, it was a flop and it cost the company a lot of money.

Now let's imagine how this event would be reacted to and interpreted by Company A, which has a culture that could be summarized as being **Performance Based**. Joe is angrily reprimanded by his superiors for taking too much risk and not doing enough research before the product was developed. Then he's fired. His direct reports are assigned to someone within the organization with more experience. People within the organization take note of what happens when someone tries something new and fails to deliver immediate positive results for the company. A PR announcement is soon released to skittish investors and the public that Joe is being replaced by a more senior manager.

Now let's imagine how this event would be reacted to and interpreted by Company B, which has a culture that could be summarized as being **Innovation Based**. A meeting is called with everyone involved in the product development and rollout. A discussion is had about what went wrong, what assumptions were probably false, and what they got right. The superiors commend everyone involved for taking a risk. It is decided that Joe will retain his position, but accept additional oversight and reorganize his team. The board is privately alerted that although the product launch failed to deliver the desired revenue, management is confident that it was a risk well worth taking, and is but one important step that will bring them closer to success.

Which company has the better culture?

I don't know. It depends on what the organization is trying to accomplish.

The appropriate company culture is one that fulfills three requirements:

1. It will assist the company in achieving its vision
2. It is conducive for effective leadership to occur
3. It does not conflict with the leader's and employees' deepest values

Every human organization will develop a distinct culture, with or without the consent of the individuals leading it. Cultures grow, become ingrained in people and in the end tremendously impact how individuals within the organization think, feel, and act. This is why it's so important to be conscious and intentional about the cultures we cultivate and become effected by. Is your company's culture complementing or killing your efforts as a leader?

Sterling Leadership Trait #22: Knows that
Money/Power Is a Means, Not an End

For what shall it profit a man, if he shall gain the
whole world, and lose his own soul?

No one sets out to lose what was once most important to them, but many do. For those in leadership roles, it is the subtle nature of money and power that often facilitates this tragic event. *Citizen Kane*, the classic Orson Welles' film released in 1941, depicts the pernicious and corrosive effects that money and power can have on those who encounter them unprepared. The film opens with the camera meandering past a NO TRESPASSING sign and into a large estate. We see all the trappings of success, now in disrepair – an empty Bengal tiger cage, Venetian style boats bobbing in the lake, a golf course green with a dilapidated sign – and an enormous mansion up on the hill. Inside, Charles Foster Kane, an immensely wealthy newspaper tycoon, is on his deathbed. He utters the word "rosebud", breathes his last, and lets a snow globe he has been clutching in his hand drop and shatter on the floor. The rest of the film follows reporter Jerry Thompson as he attempts to learn the significance of Kane's last word. By interviewing those who used to be close to Kane, Thompson is able to piece together Kane's impoverished early childhood, the wealth his family stumbled into, his initial journalistic idealism and his eventual blind pursuit of wealth and power that led to the destruction of all his relationships and his complete undoing.

Although Thompson is unable to find out what "rosebud" was, he reaches the conclusion that:

> *Mr. Kane was a man who got everything he wanted, and then lost it. Maybe rosebud was something he couldn't get, or something he lost.*

There's nothing inherently wrong with a desire for fine things and ambition. But there was something deeply wrong with Kane's belief regarding what those things would bring him. In biblical terms, they became idols, which he served diligently. Their only command was that he accumulate more. More money. More power. More things. And they had to be acquired and consumed in greater and greater amounts. In obedience to his idols, Kane sacrificed every relationship he had and trampled on every good belief he once held. He became whatever he had to be in order to serve his idols and in the end he was left with nothing of worth but a memory of a goodness long gone, symbolized by a sled from his childhood named *Rosebud*. Kane had gained the world, and in the process he had lost his soul.

Money and power are excellent tools for obtaining legitimate goals – but, the blind pursuit of money and power in and of themselves leaves us with nothing of lasting value. Kane only realized this error as he lay dying. It turns out that the pursuit of money and power are not only seductive, but phenomenally distracting from what matters in life, right up to the end. Death, on the other hand, as Kane discovered to his horror, has a way of evaporating the perceived worth of massive empires, fame, caged exotic animals, golf courses, and boats. Surviving an encounter with wealth and power will require each of us to reject the self-centered and self-serving philosophy Kane lived by.

So, how else can and should we live? You, as a leader, have the added responsibility to tackle this question because how you answer it will impact not only yourself, but those whom you lead. Early Greek thinkers like Plato and Aristotle committed a tremendous amount of time and energy attempting to answer this question and today we can benefit from the mental heavy lifting that they did all those centuries ago. Aristotle, perceiving that all humans seek personal fulfillment in various ways, classified them into a hierarchy of three levels. Each level is a different way of seeking personal fulfillment.

Laetus (Immediate Gratification)

Laetus is the most basic level of personal fulfillment. Individuals operating at this level are seeking to maximize pleasure and minimize pain, with little thought of the future. This type of personal fulfillment is as quickly and easily gained as it is lost. When we operate only on this level we do not consider how our decisions will impact those around us. We soon regret many of these decisions. Making decisions based *only* on immediate gratification is an immature and yet, at times, tempting way to live.

Felix (Personal Achievement)

This means of personal fulfillment takes more time, effort, and struggle to attain. The fulfillment from achieving something at this level, such as saving up for a down payment for a house or finally getting a promotion, lasts longer than Laetus, but is just as self-centered, and ultimately is equally as fleeting.

Beatitudinal (Good Beyond Self)

The Beatitudinal type of personal fulfillment happens when we put the needs and desires of others before our own and choose to pursue the greater good. This type of personal fulfillment is not dependent on whether the good thing that we have done is recognized or not, or even whether it is in conflict with our personal interest. When we do the right thing for the right reason for the benefit of others, we transcend the cold calculus of selfish human behavior and give the cynics pause. Finding personal fulfillment through Beatitudinal acts does not fade and in the long run is never regretted.

It is important to realize that seeking immediate gratification is not always bad and neither is personal achievement. In fact, both of those types of personal fulfillment can sometimes be pursued without harming others and may be necessary in order do a Beatitudinal act. However, if you as a leader are only operating at the Laetus and Felix levels, you will fail. Our best leaders, every last one of them, believed in and worked towards a goal that was greater than their personal ambition or self-gratification. They saw money and power as a means but not an end.

Acknowledgements

Writing a book is never a solo project. I am deeply indebted to my wonderful son Michael for his help in interpreting my thoughts related to the leadership coaching process here at Sterling Integrators, Inc. My wife Sally has been a constant and unwavering source of inspiration and support throughout the development of our guiding principles especially in those formative years when the name "Sterling Integrators" emerged as a key descriptor of the corporate mission.

      I would like to bring special attention to the two crucial people who were foundational in my personal and professional development. First, my father, Rolf Hendrick Beerhorst, who provided a "sterling" example of Christianity in action where word and deed were practiced throughout my life. He showed me that there was never a right way to do the wrong thing and that the true measure of a person was what they did when no one was watching. Dad, I will be forever grateful for your shining example!

And I would also like to acknowledge my first boss, Miervaldis (Bill) Paberzs, who taught me what true leadership looked like in the workplace, where a job well done meant the customer would be satisfied and that customer would in turn spread the word to others  about quality workmanship. Bill never believed in "shortcuts" but rather taught me the "why" first and then the "what" and then finally the "how" which led the way to satisfaction in a finished project. Thank you Bill for being a truly great teacher by being the example of "integration" of mind/heart/hands in the workplace!

Notes

[1] PricewaterhouseCoopers (PwC). *Engaging and Empowering Millennials: A follow-up to PwC's NextGen global generational study*. pwc.com. 2014.

[2] Matt Symonds. "Executive coaching - another set of clothes for the Emperor?" *Forbes*. forbes.com. January 2011.

[3] Carol Kauffman and Diane Coutu. "The Realities of Executive Coaching." *HBR Research Report*. January 2009.

[4] I owe the inspiration for my discussion of the three H's (Hungry, Hone-able, and Honorable) to Orrin Woodward and Chris Brady. See especially their book Launching a Leadership Revolution (Obstaclés Press, 2013) page 26 and following.

[5] Jim Collins. "The Misguided Mix-up of Celebrity and Leadership" jimcollins.com. September/October 2001.

[6] Frank Acland. "Lockheed Martin's Skunk Works Shooting for 100 MW Fusion Prototype by 2017." *E-Cat World*. February 2013.

[7] Sophie Novack. "The Next Frontier for 3-D Printing: Human Organs." *National Journal*. www.nationaljournal.com. December 2013.

[8] Jo Best. "IBM Watson: The inside Story of How the Jeopardy-Winning Supercomputer Was Born, and What It Wants to Do next - Feature." *TechRepublic*. techrepublic.com. September 2013.

[9] Ashlee Vance. "Illumina's DNA Supercomputer Ushers in the $1,000 Human Genome." *Bloomberg Business*. bloomberg.com. January 2014.

[10] Signe Brewster. "What Is Graphene? Here's What You Need to Know about a Material That

Could Be the next Silicon." *Gigaom*. gigaom.com
January 2013.

Made in the USA
Lexington, KY
29 July 2017